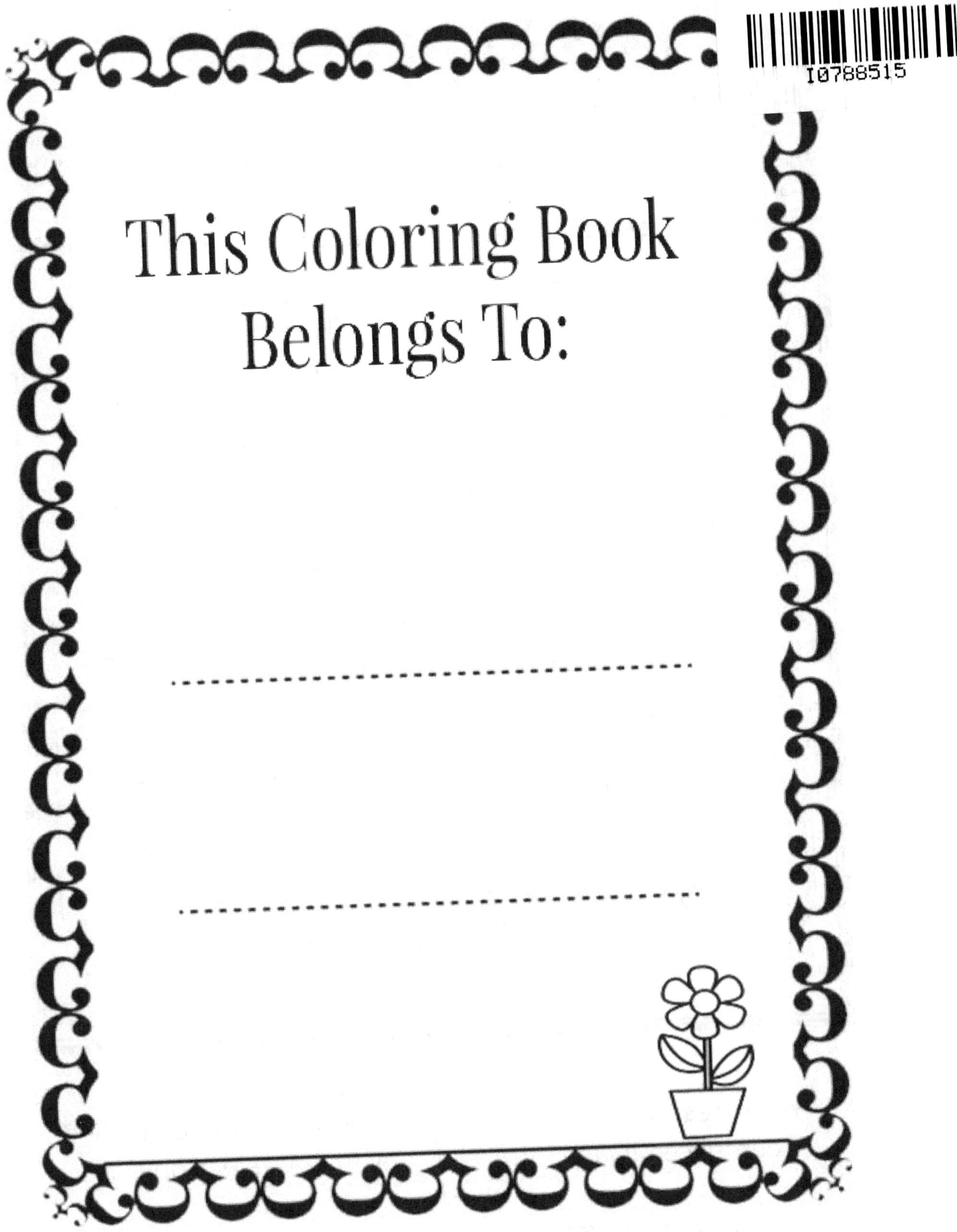

This Coloring Book
Belongs To:

INTERIOR DESIGN

COLORING BOOK

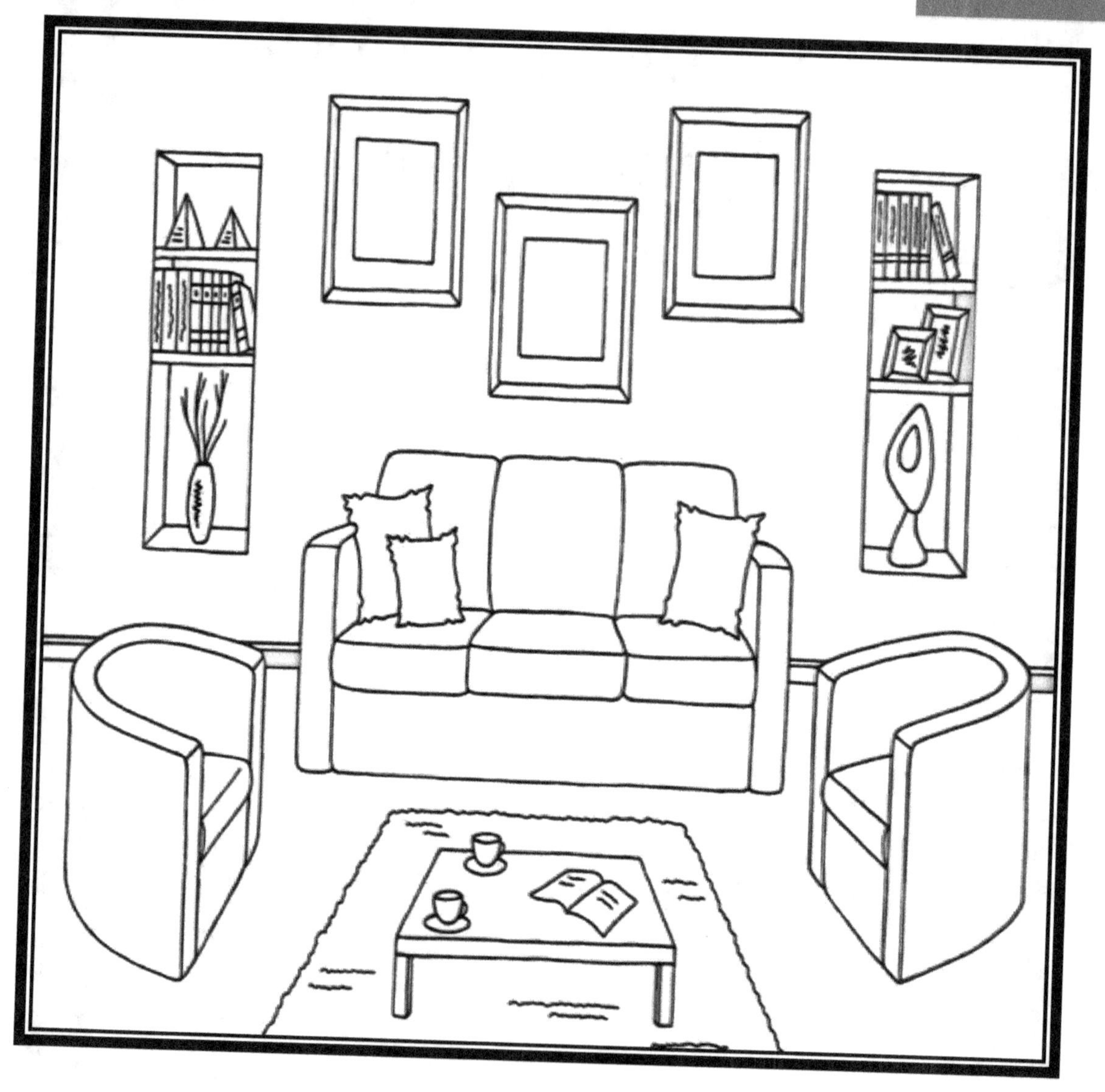

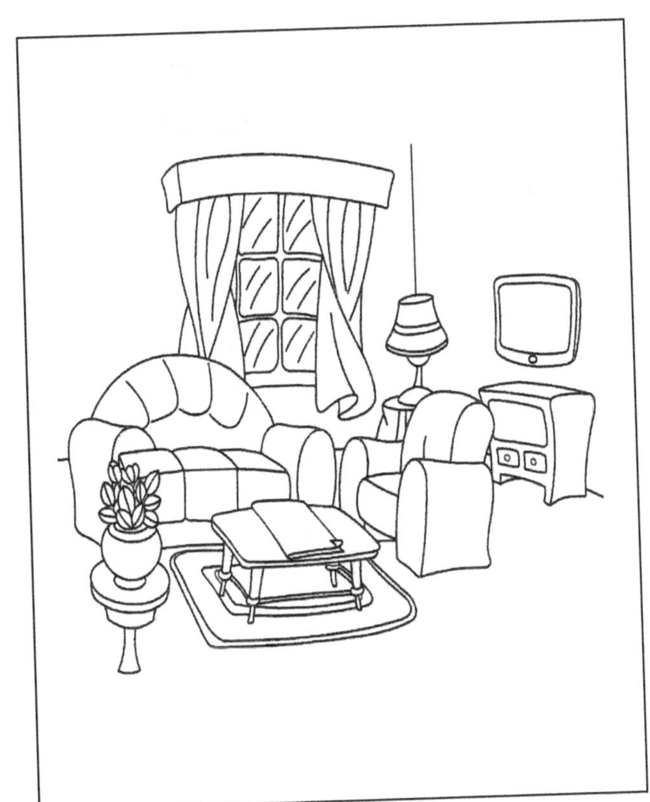
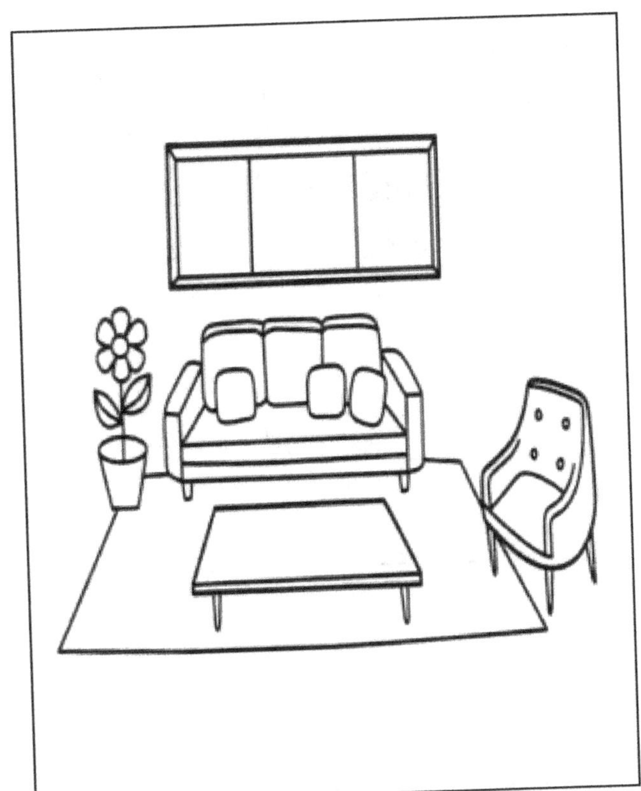
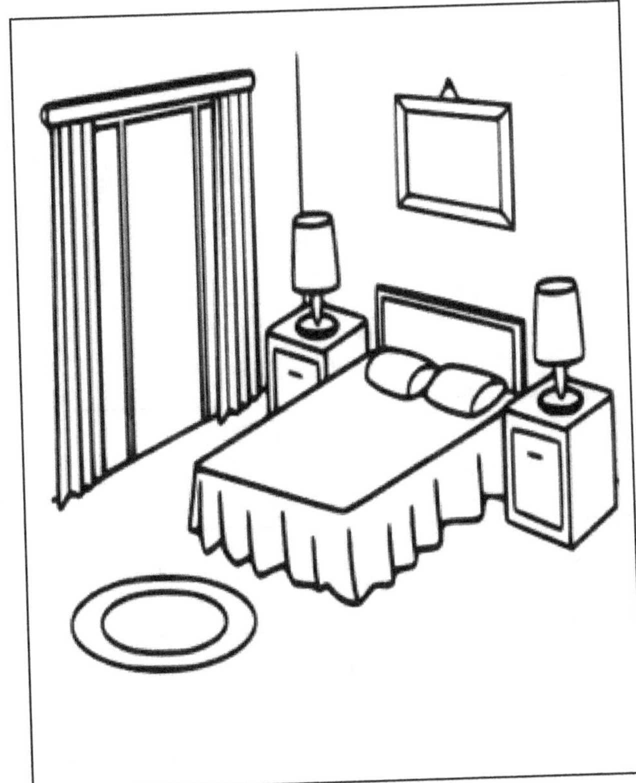
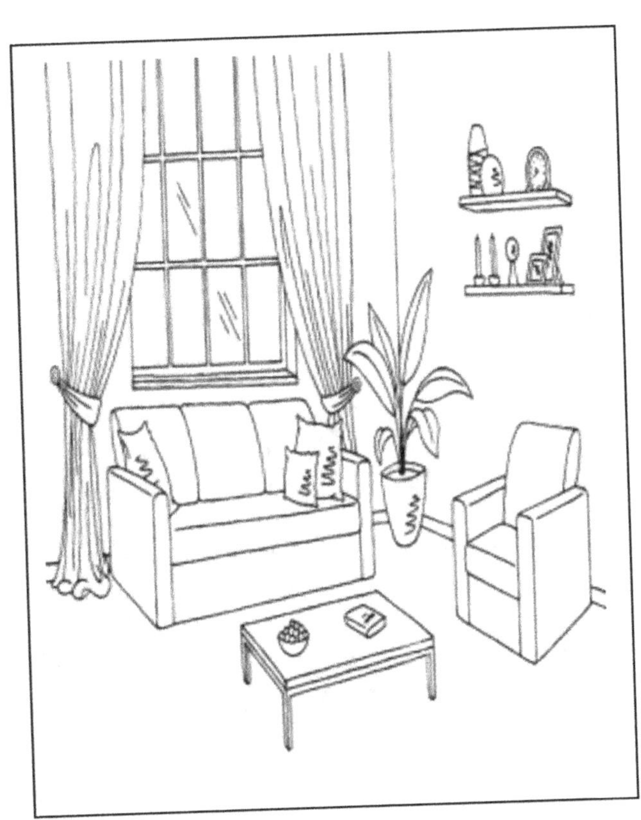

TEST COLOR PAGE

CHECK HOW YOUR COLORS SHOW OUR PAPER HERE

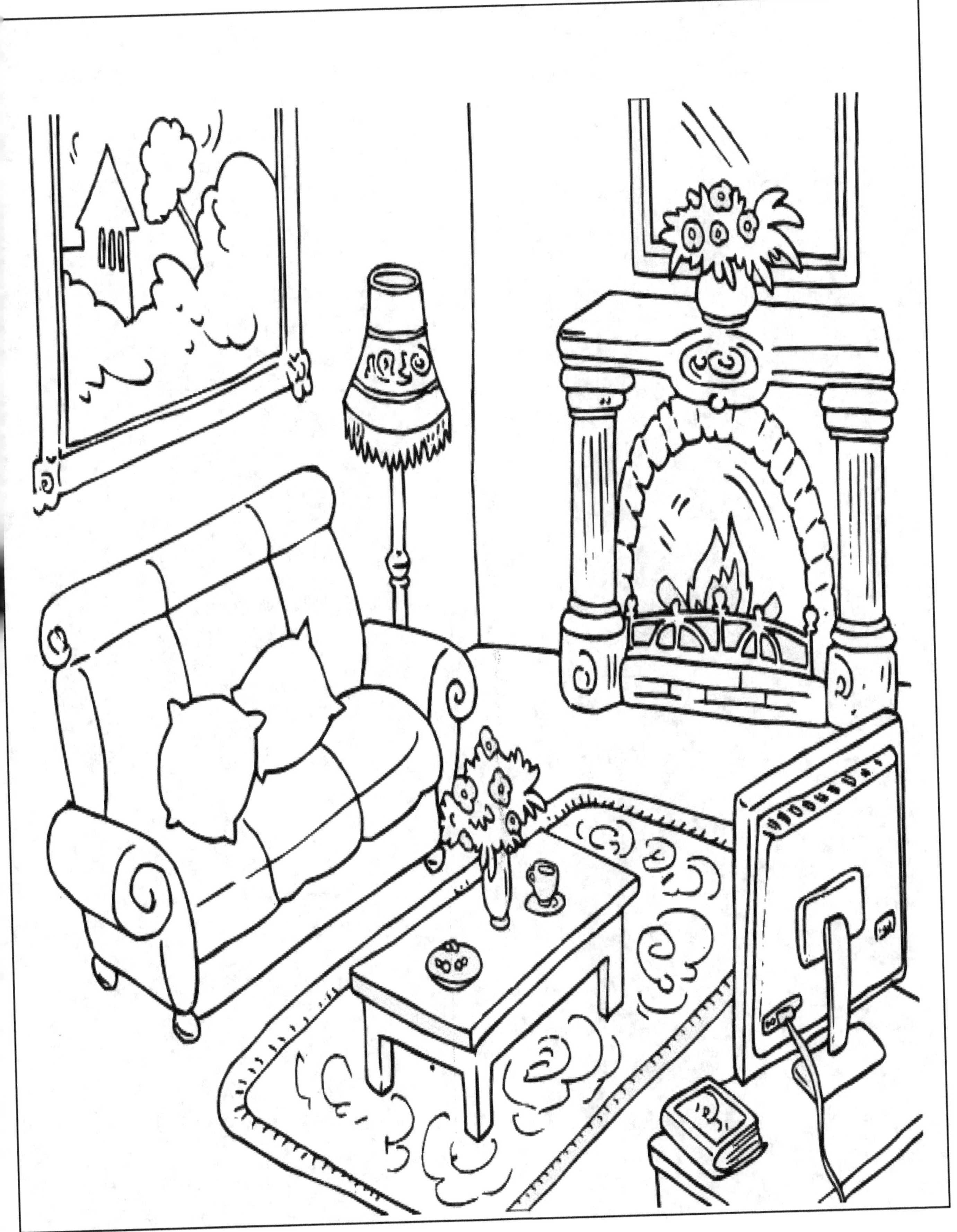

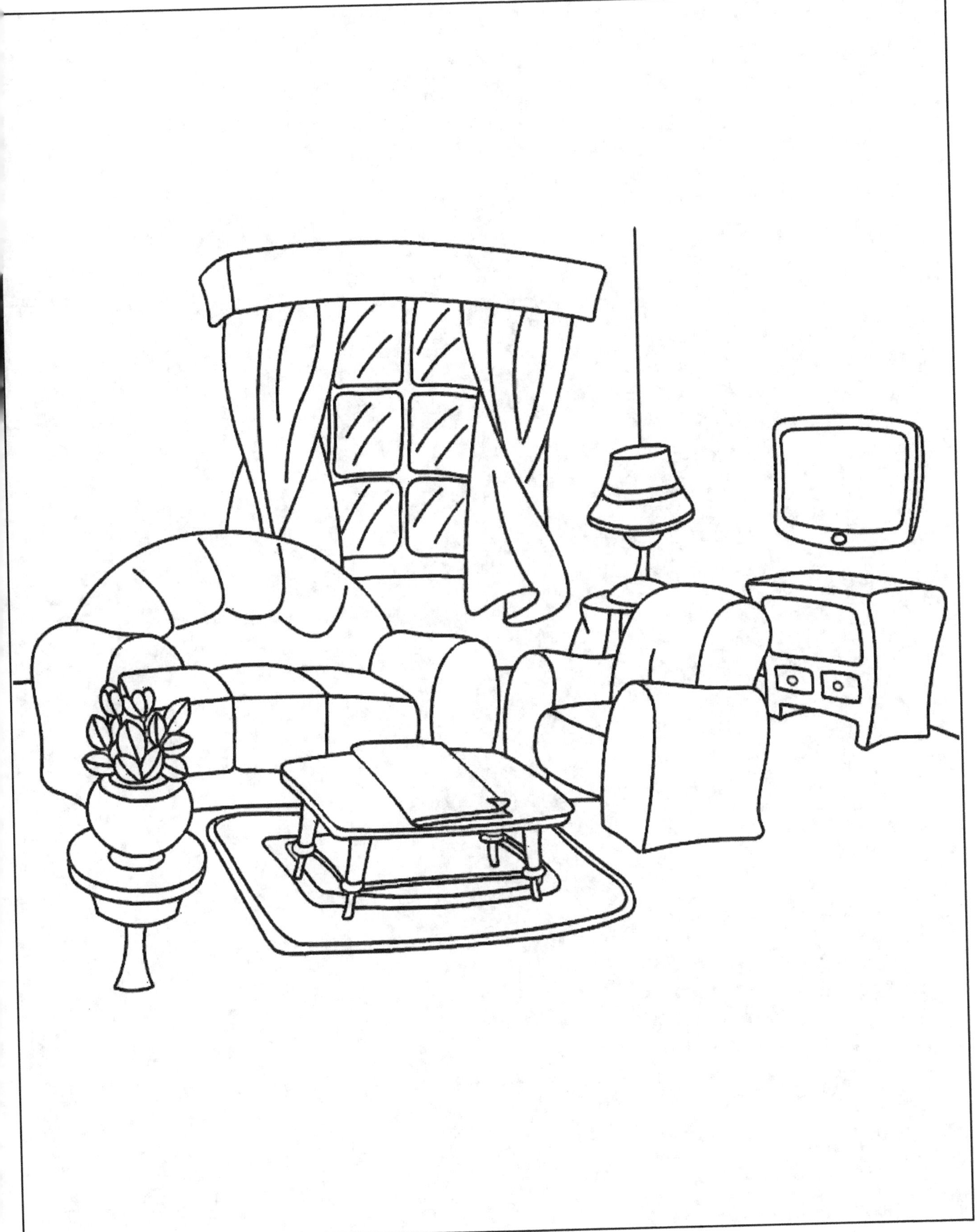

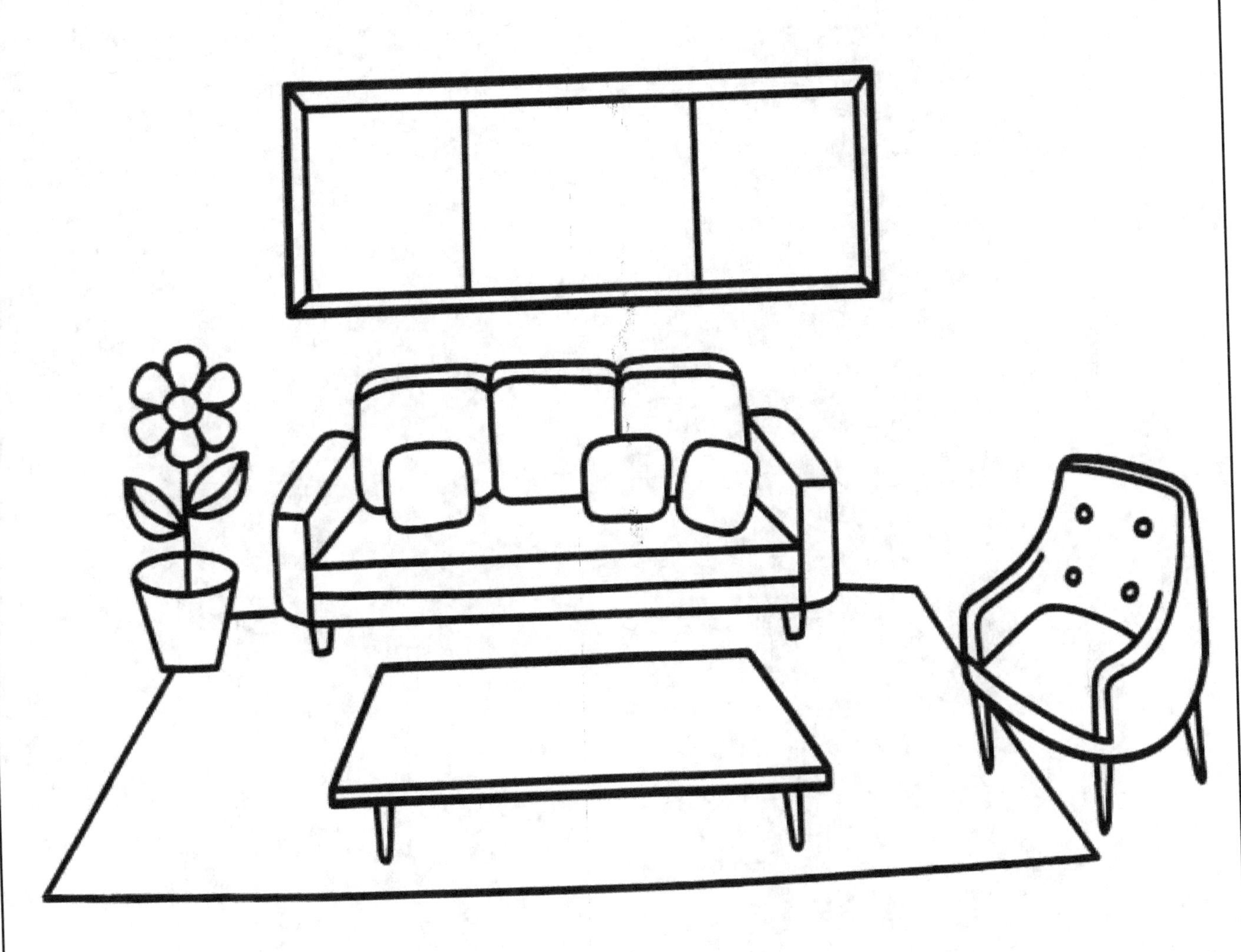

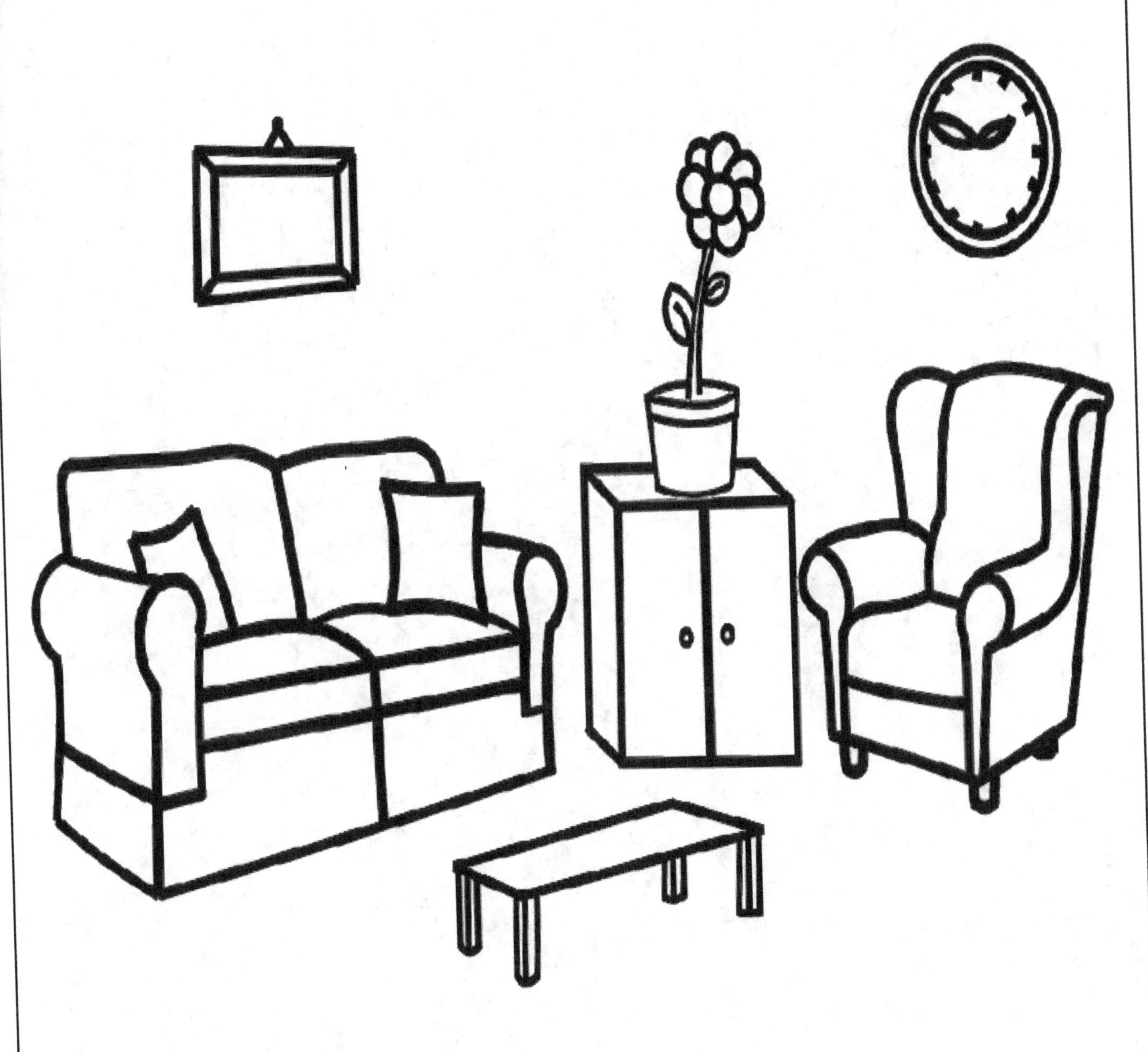

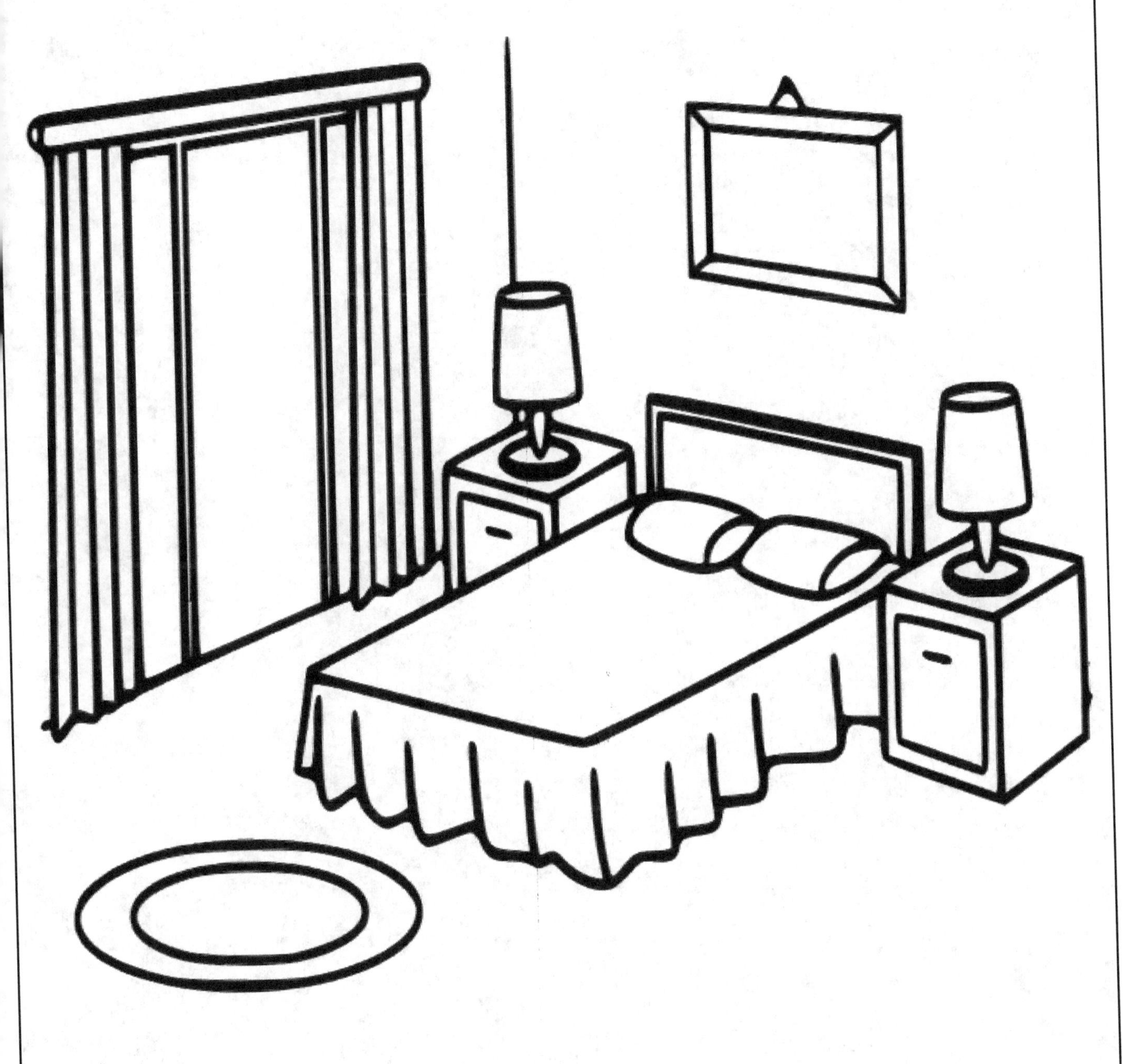

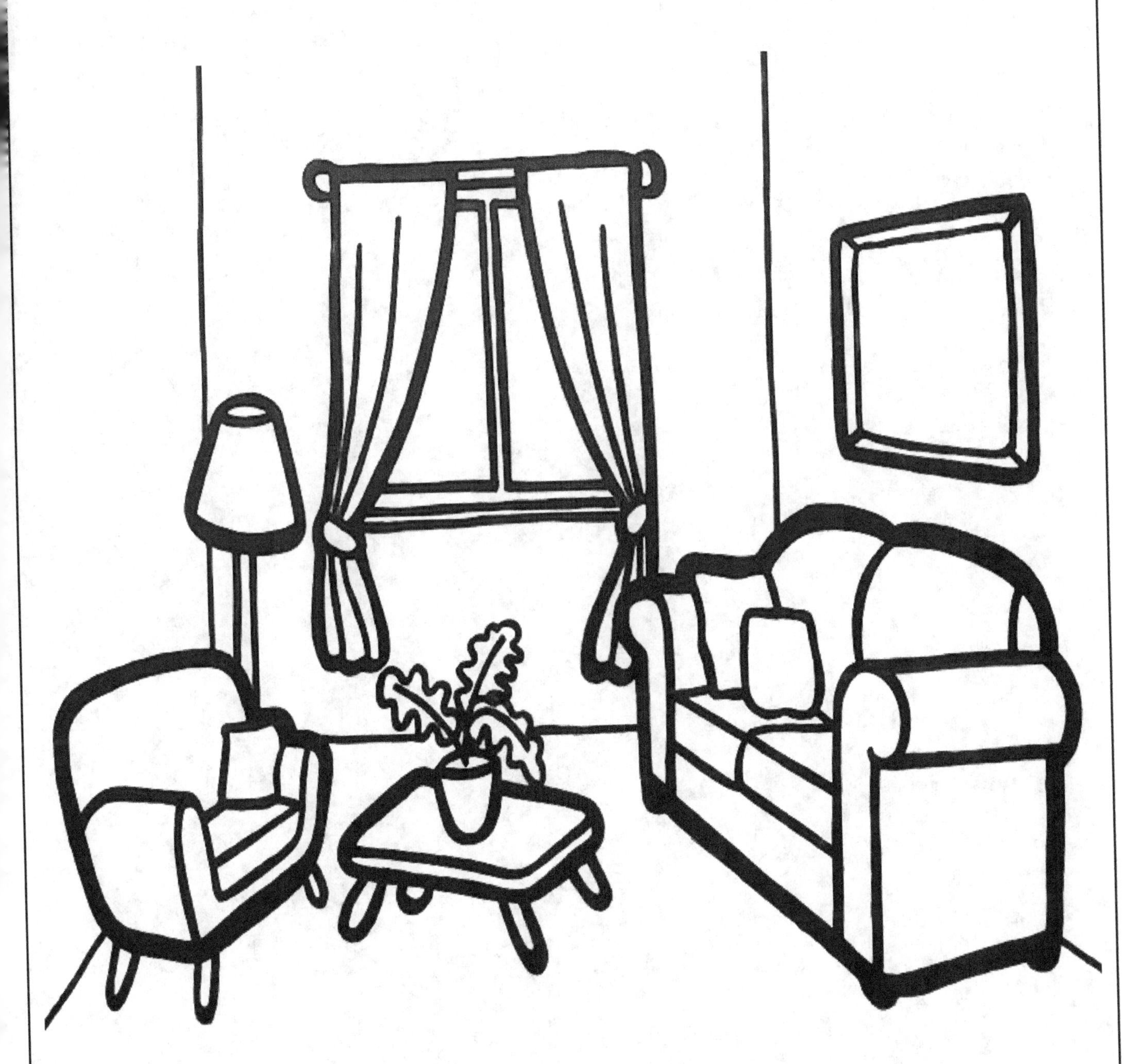

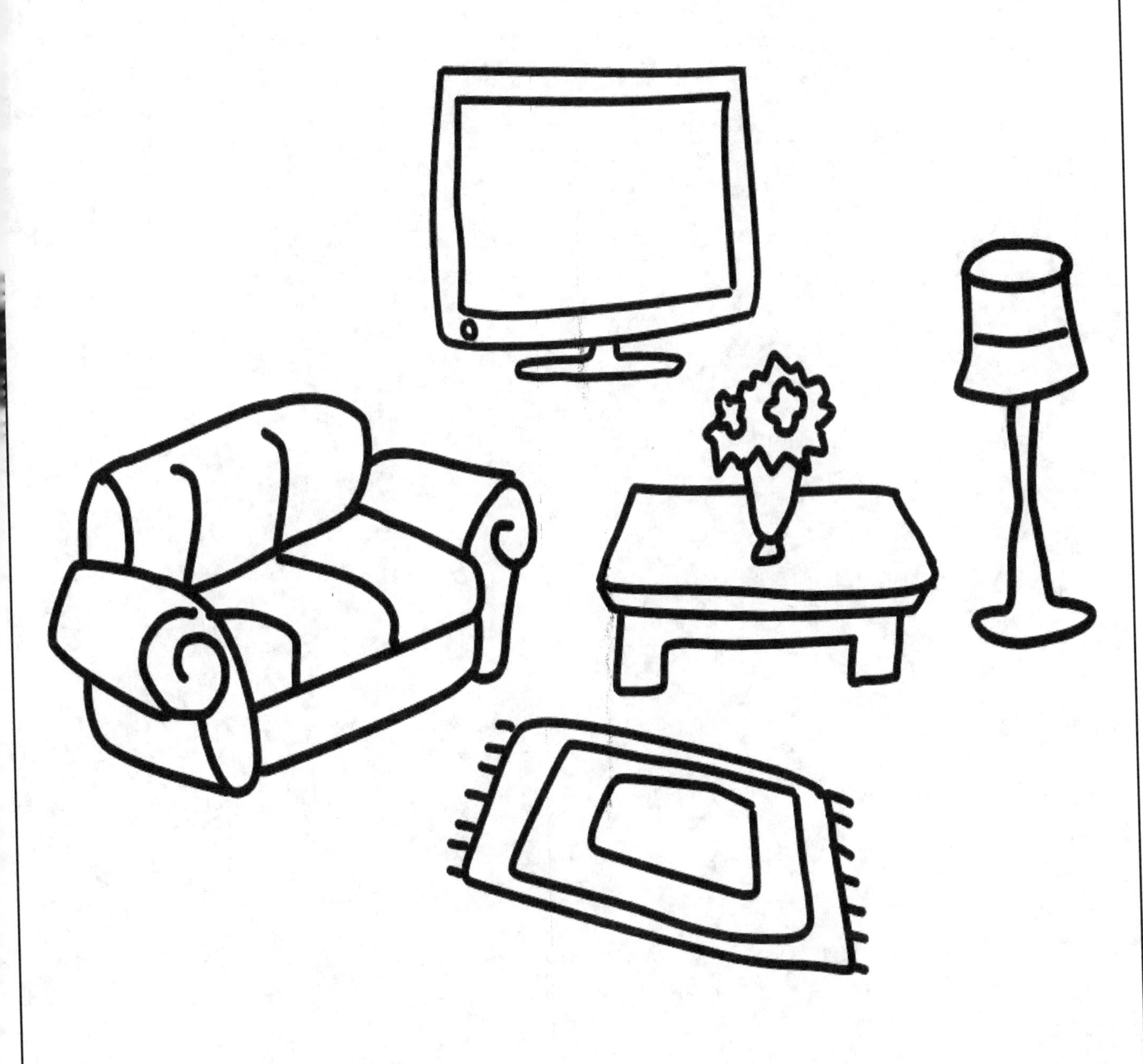

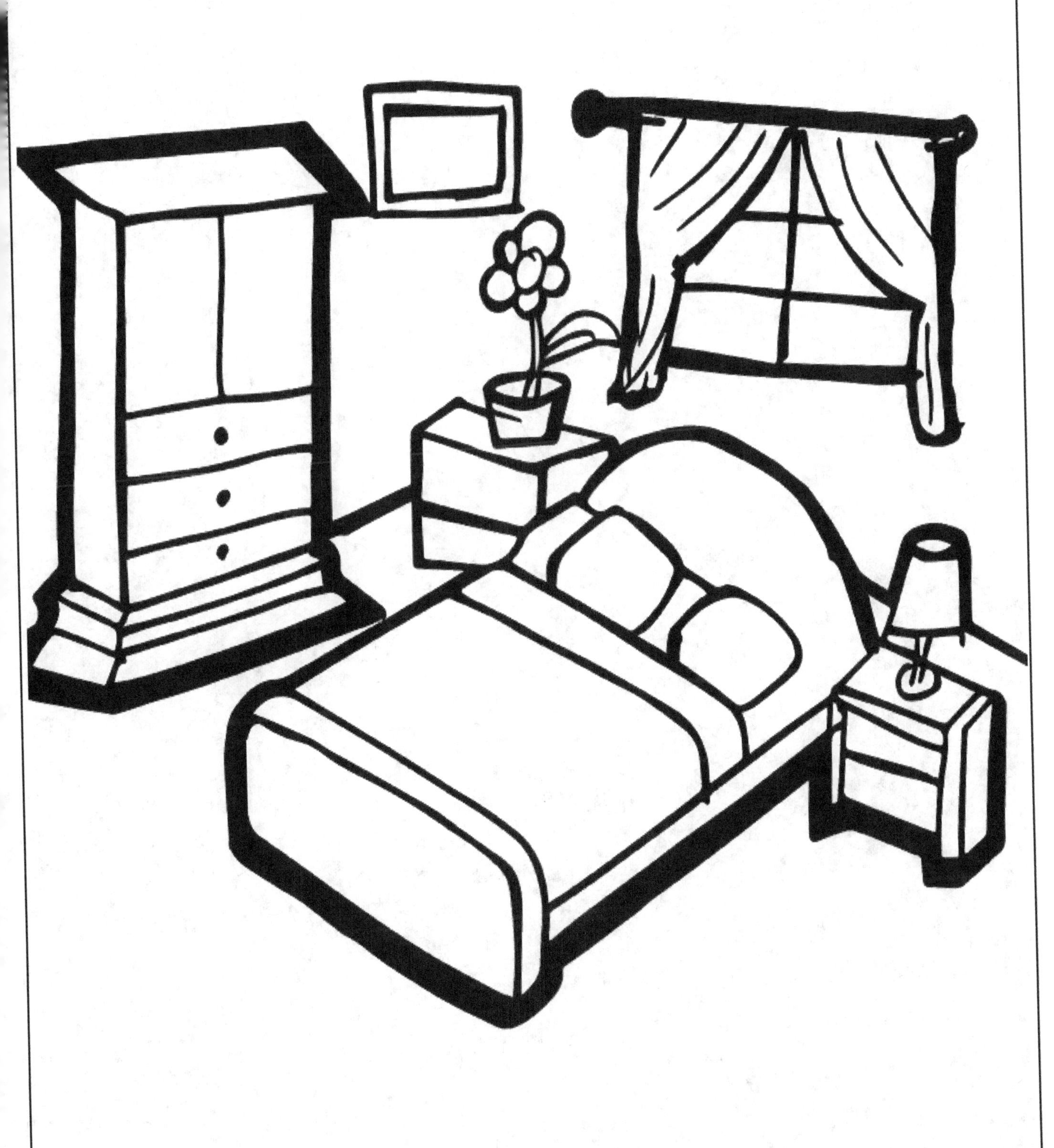

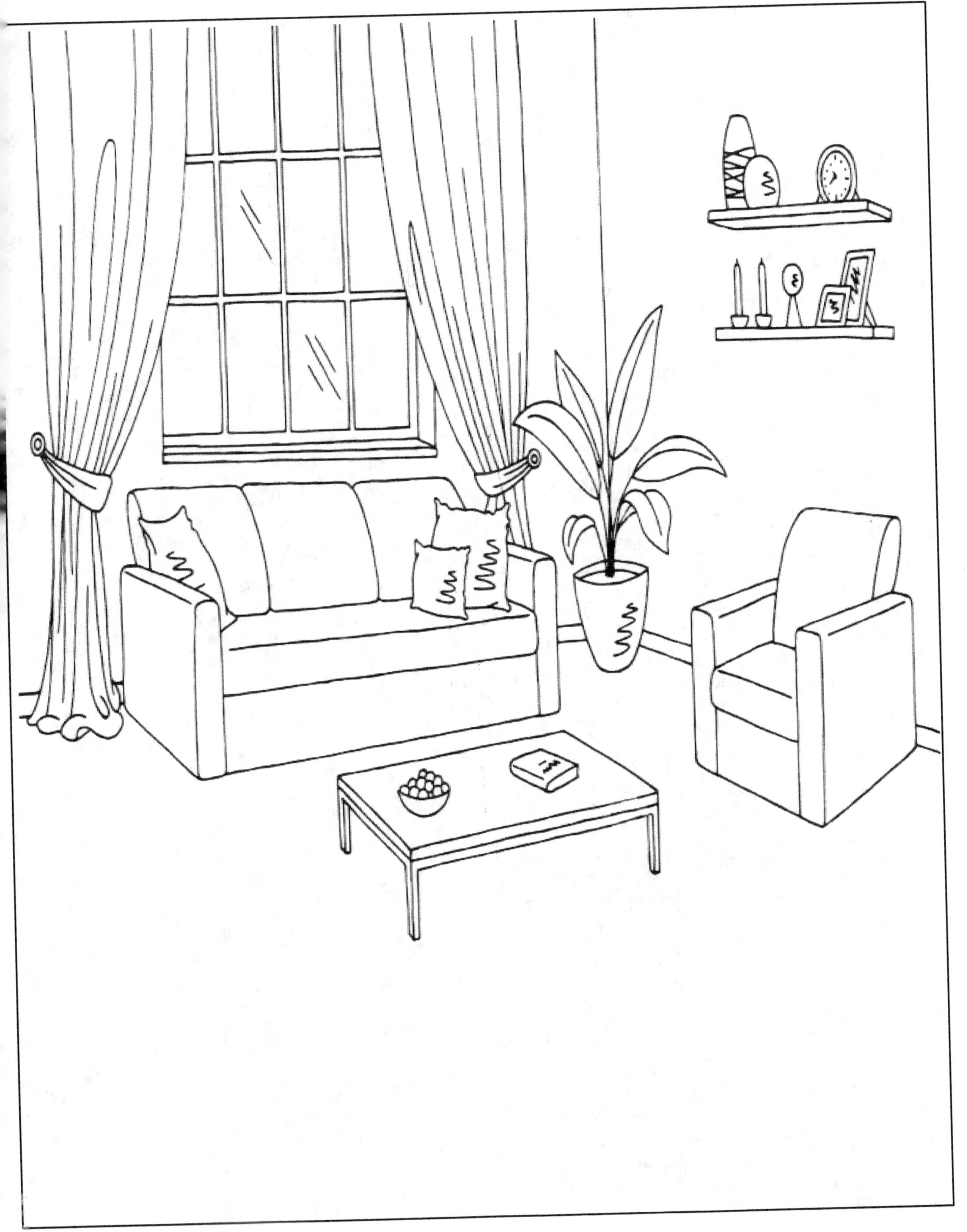

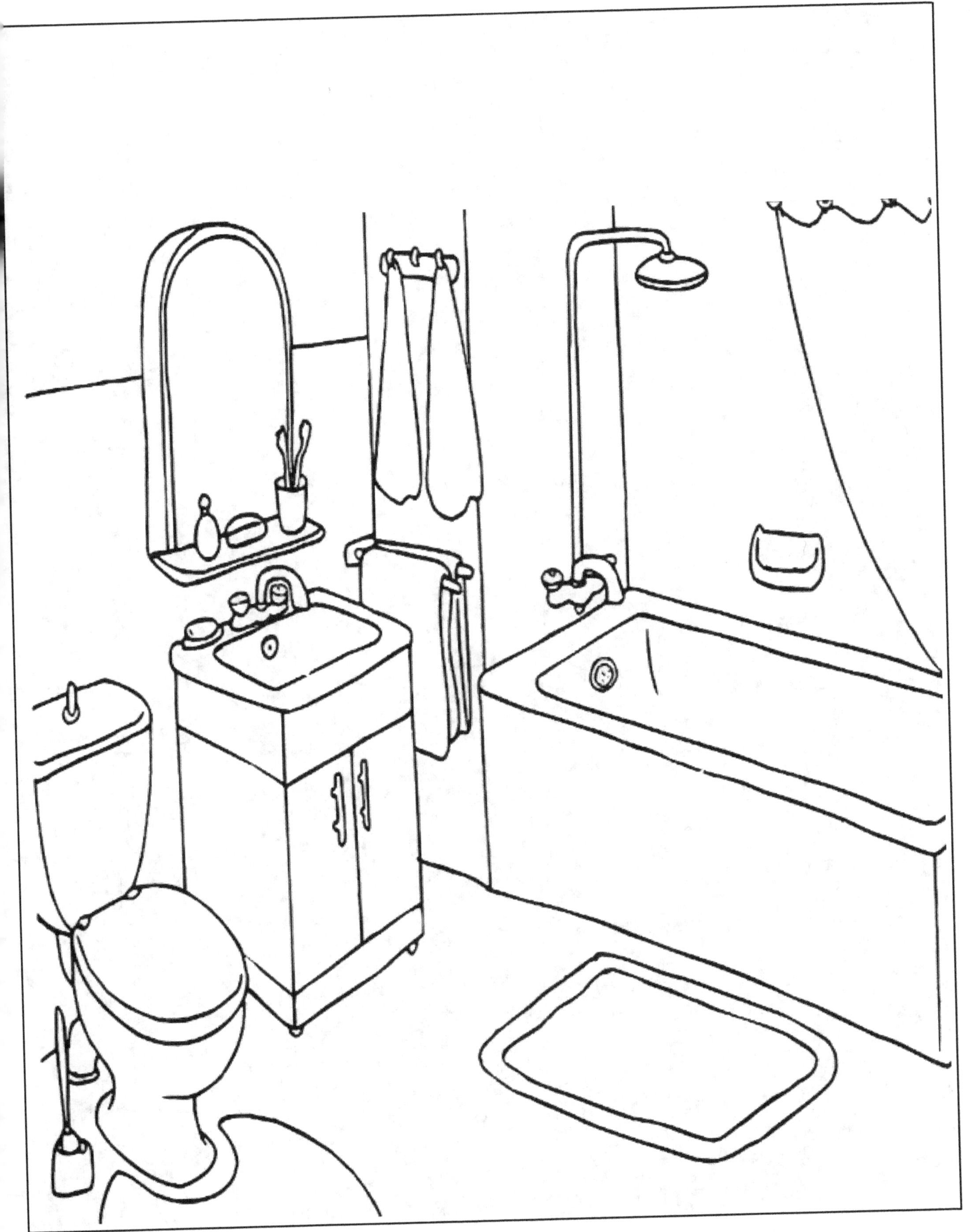

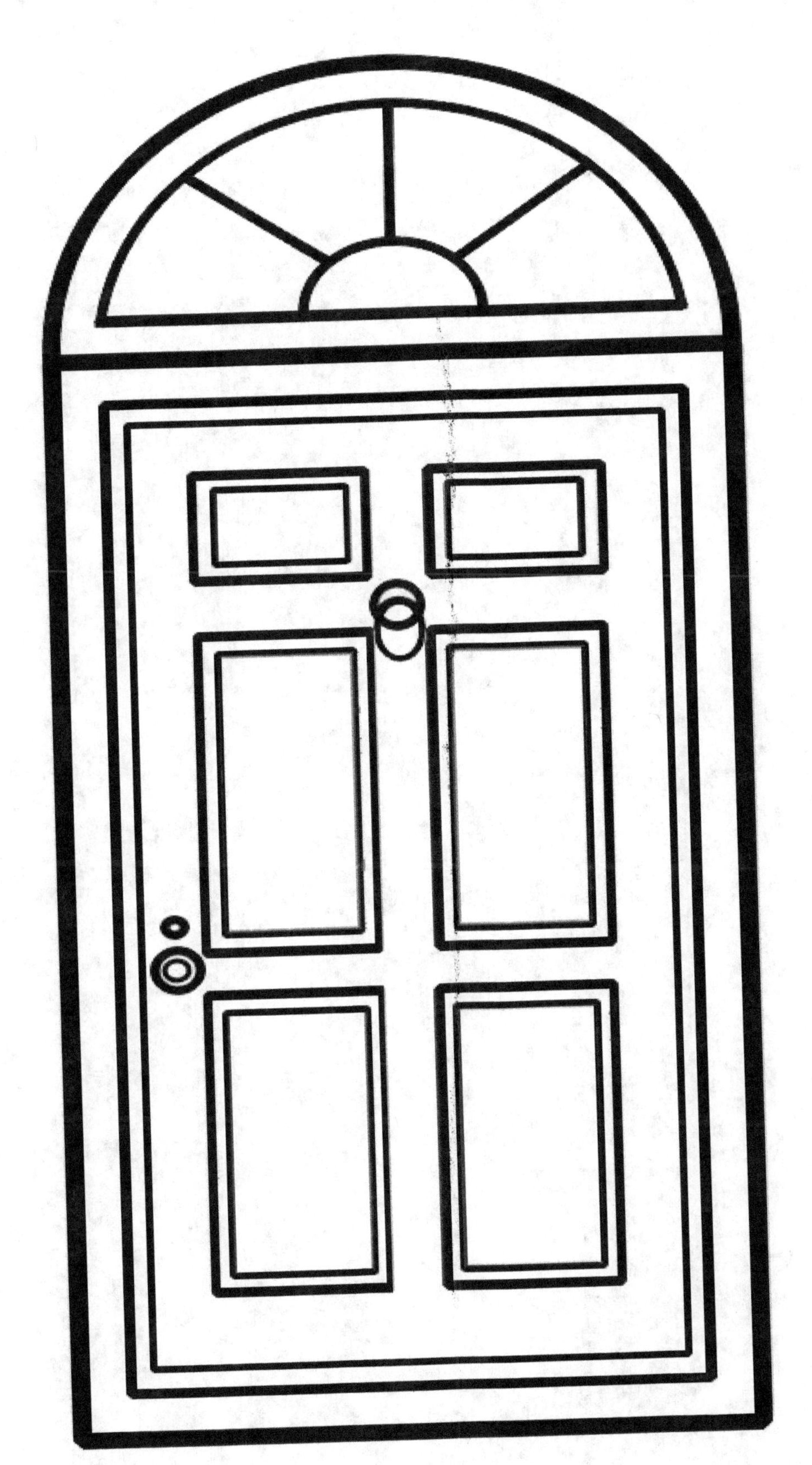

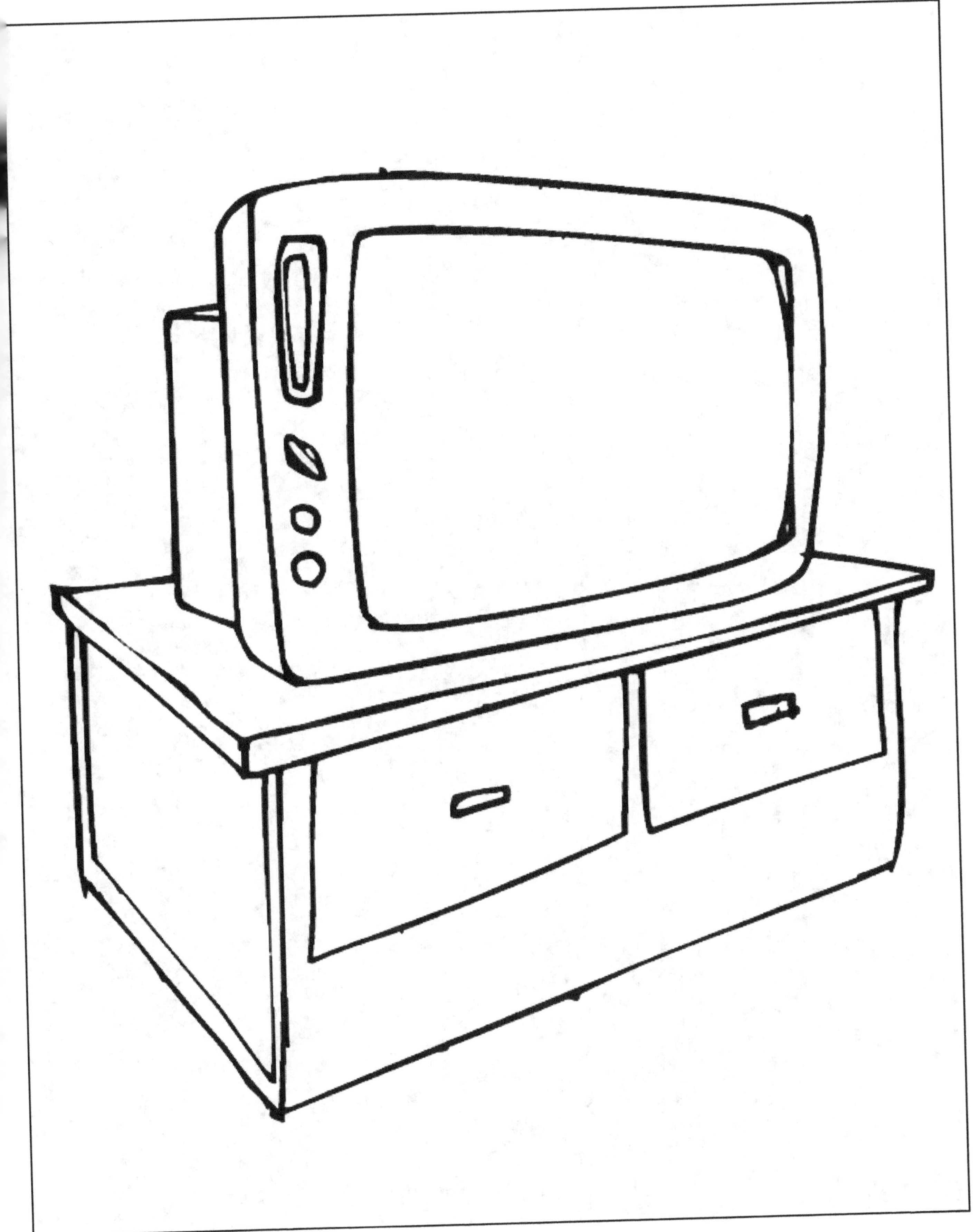

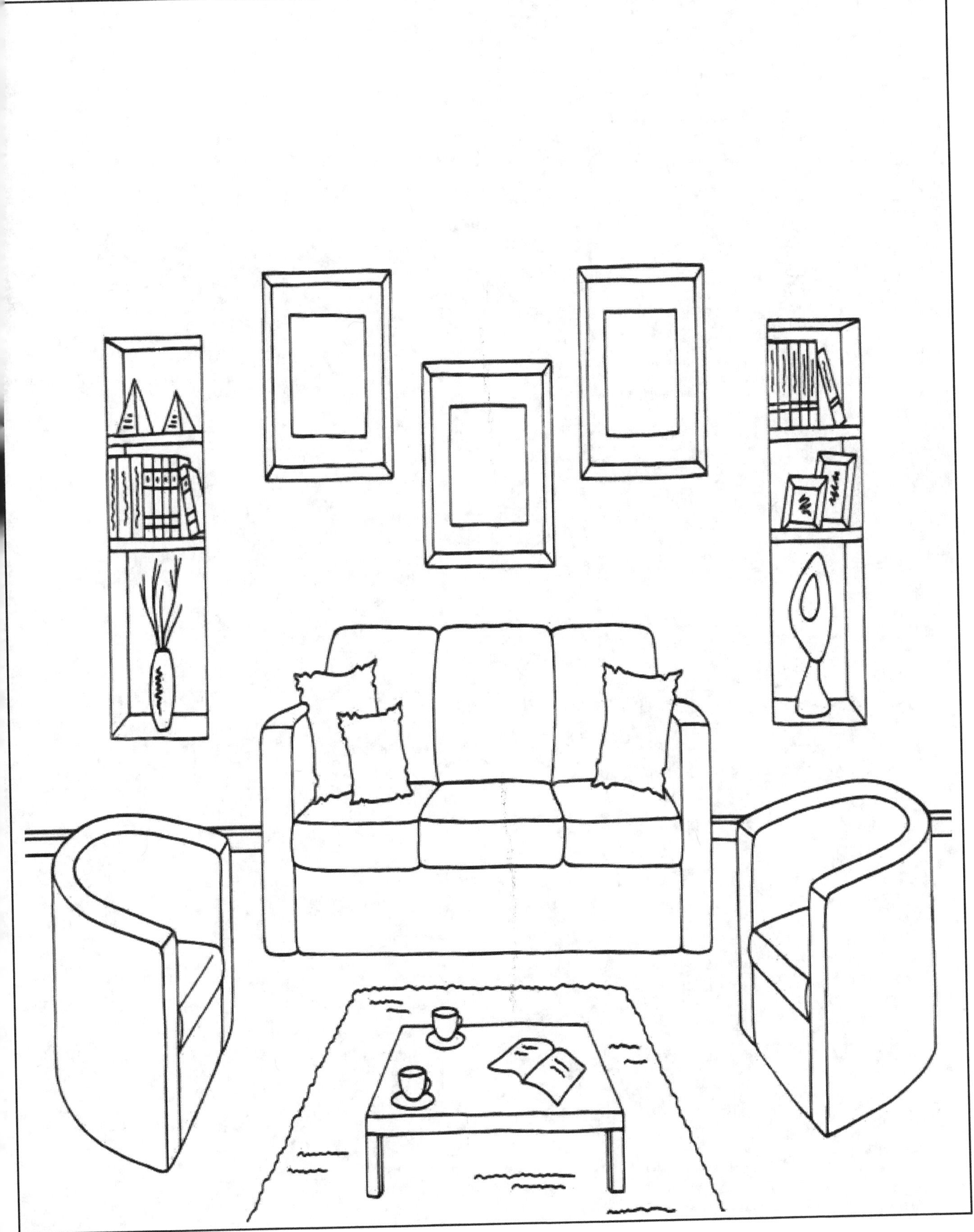

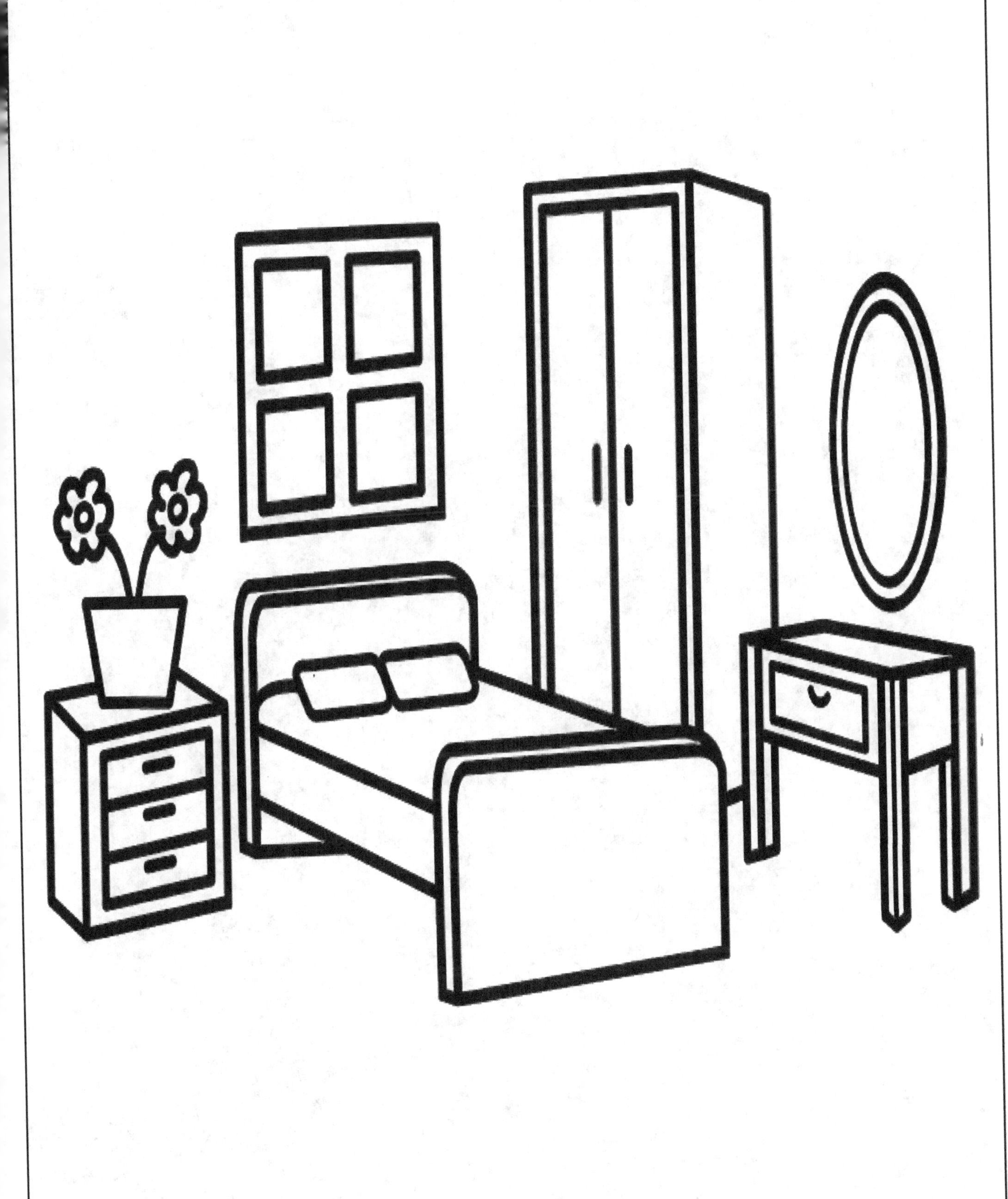

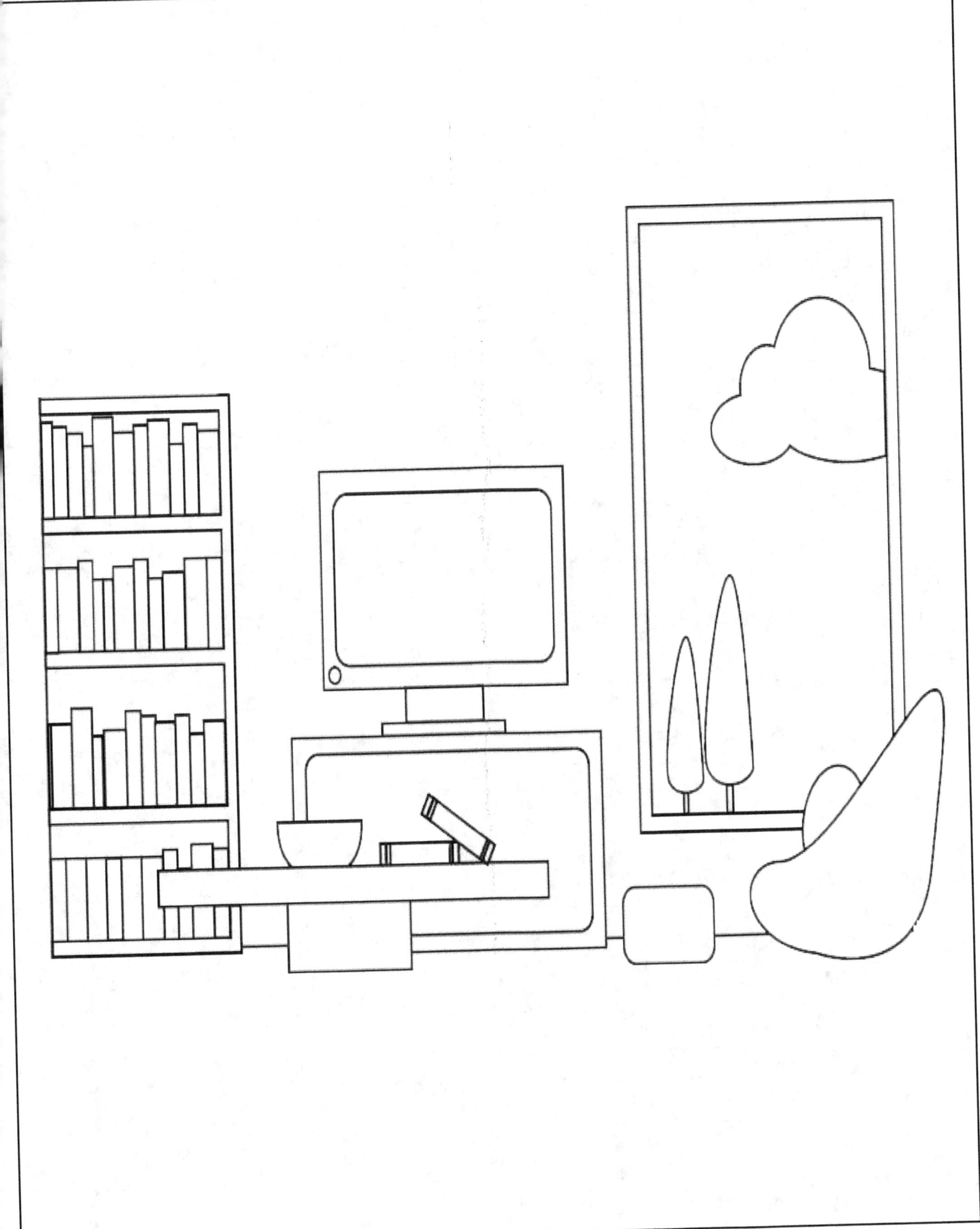

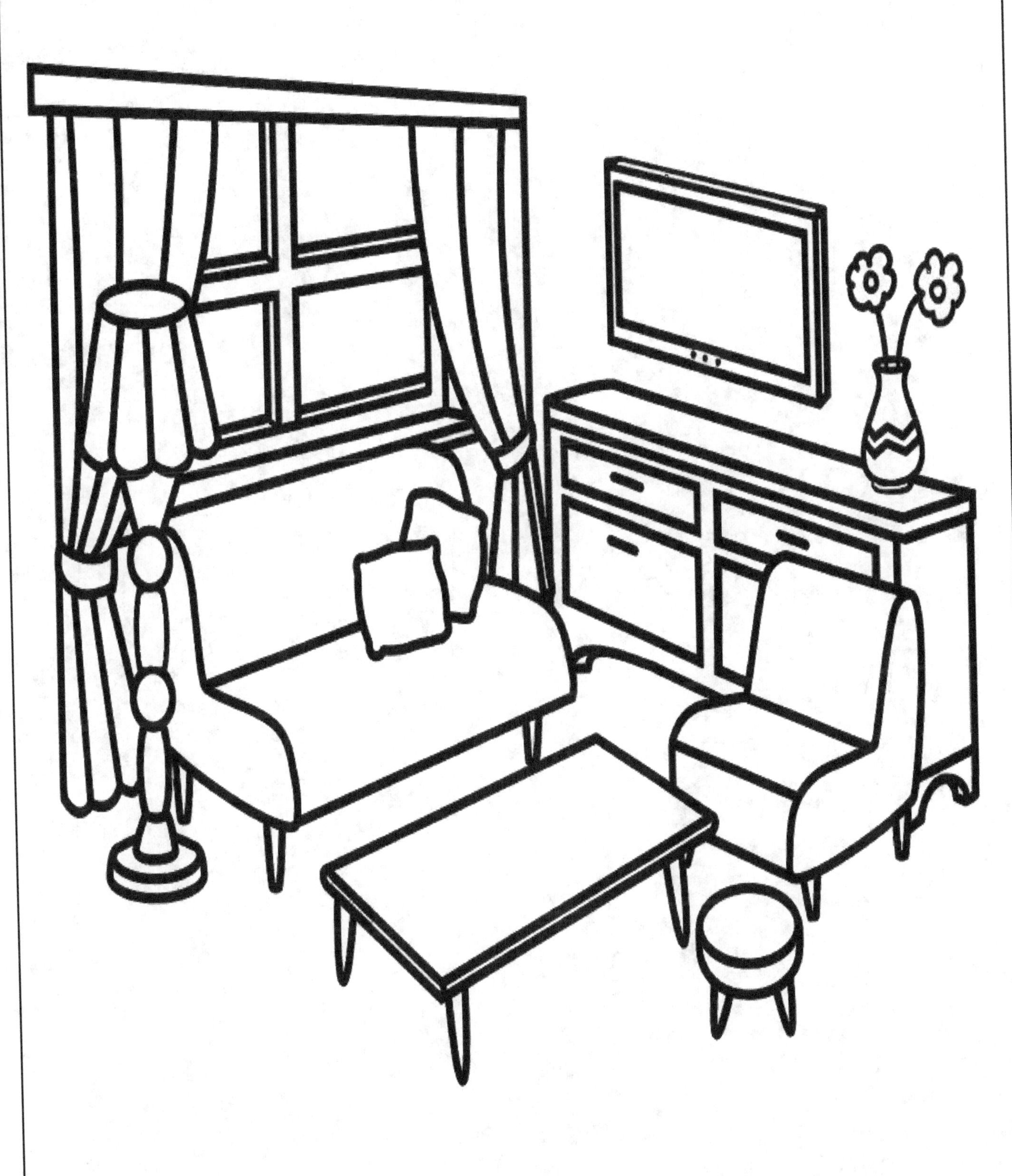

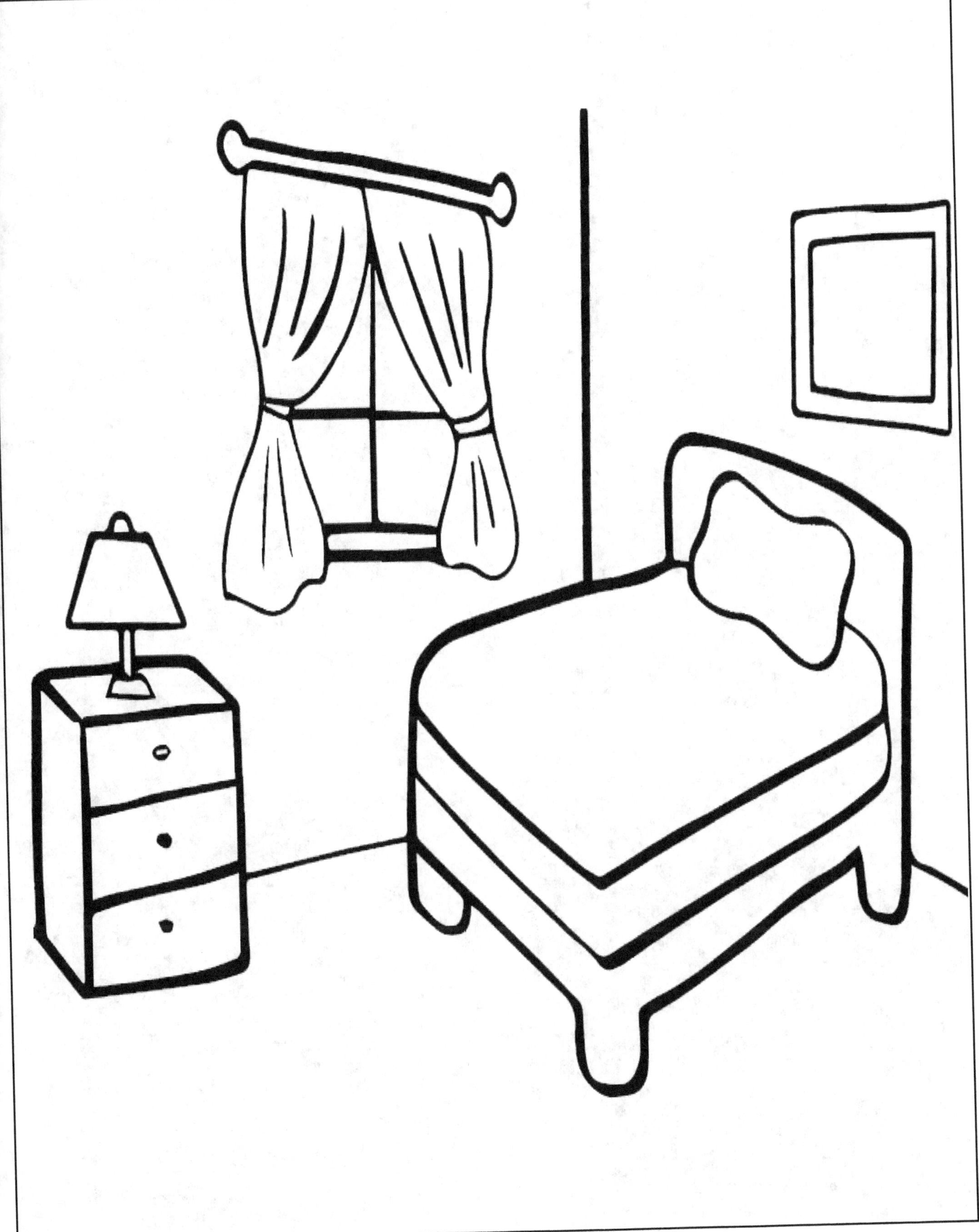

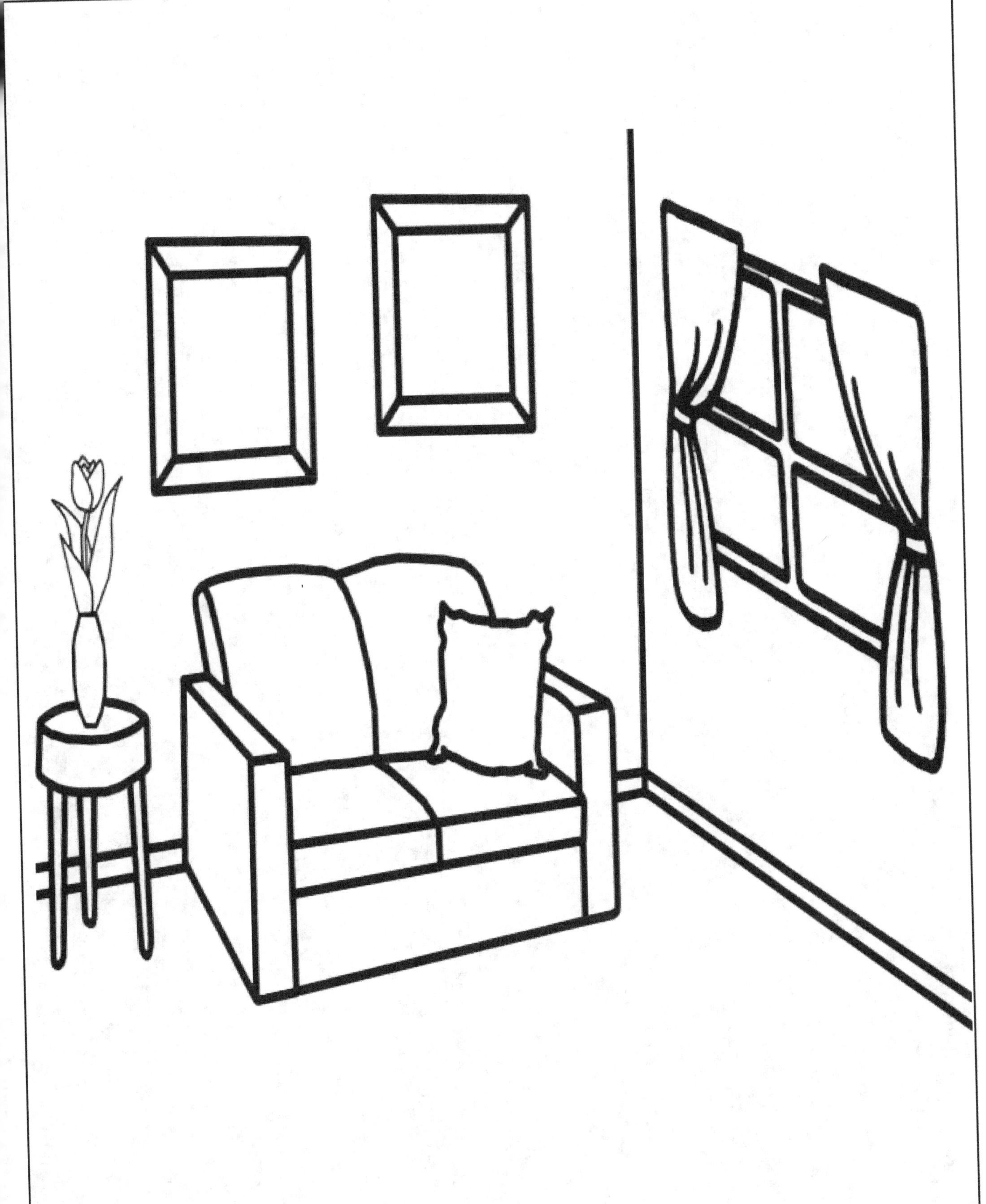

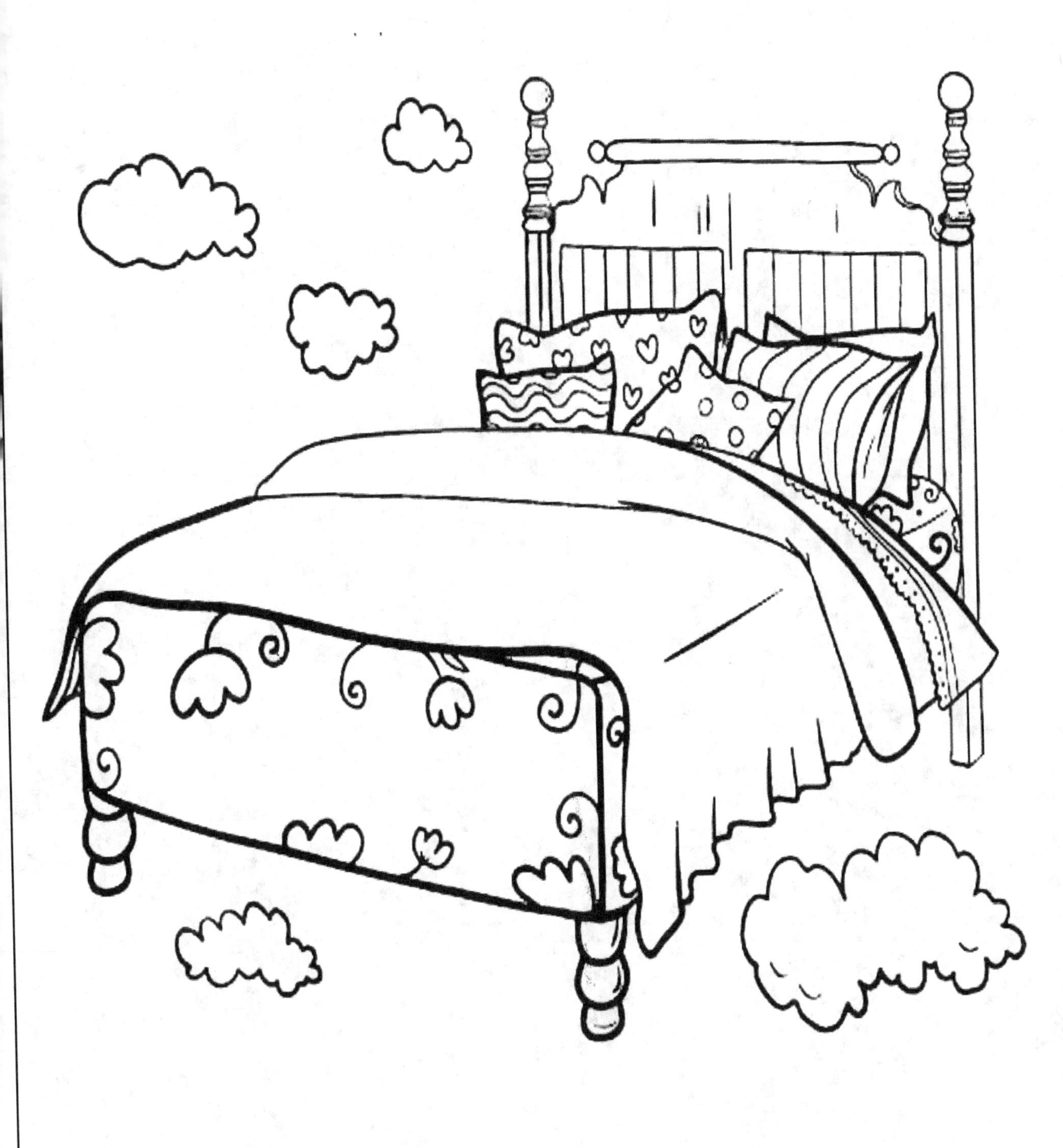

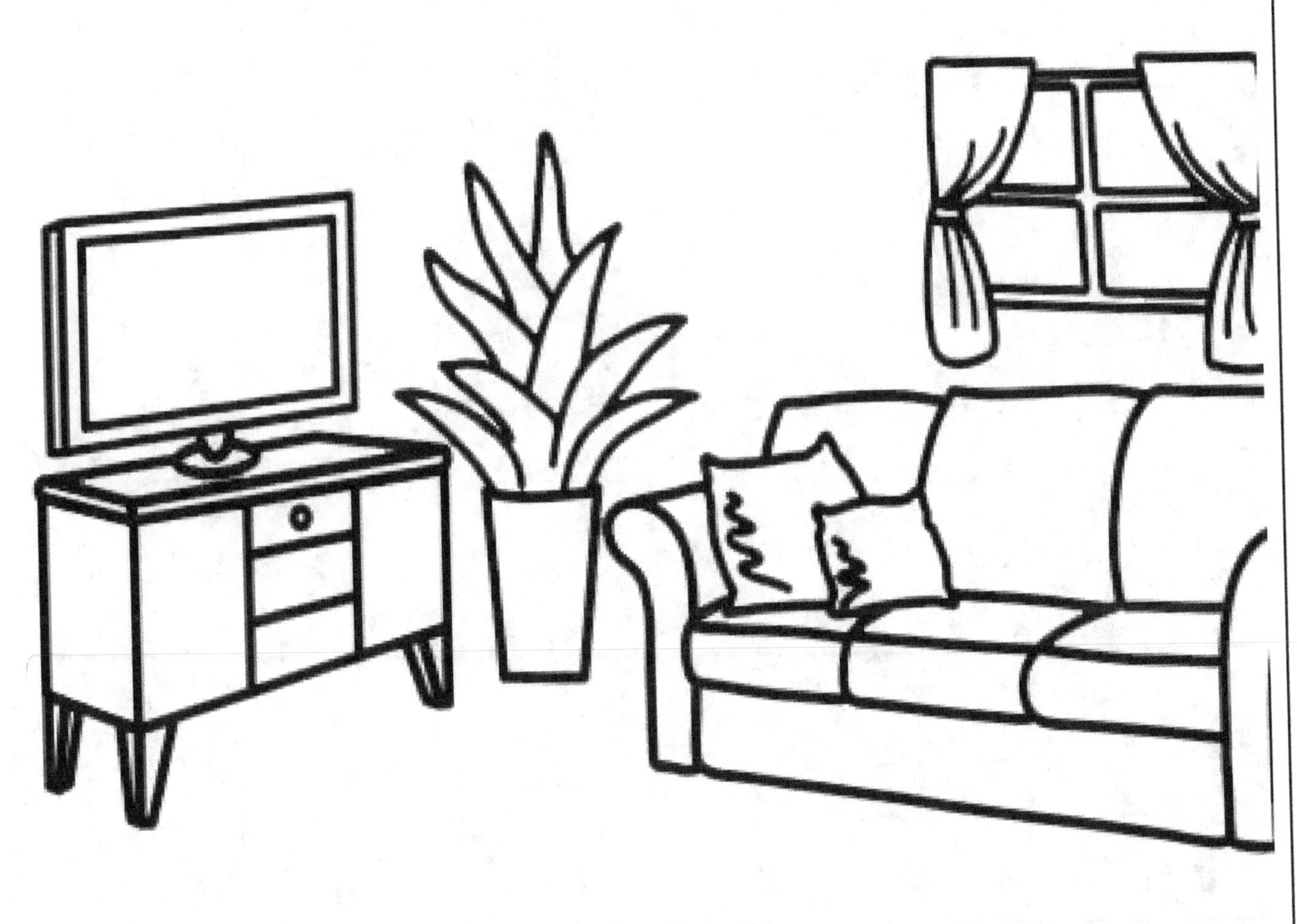

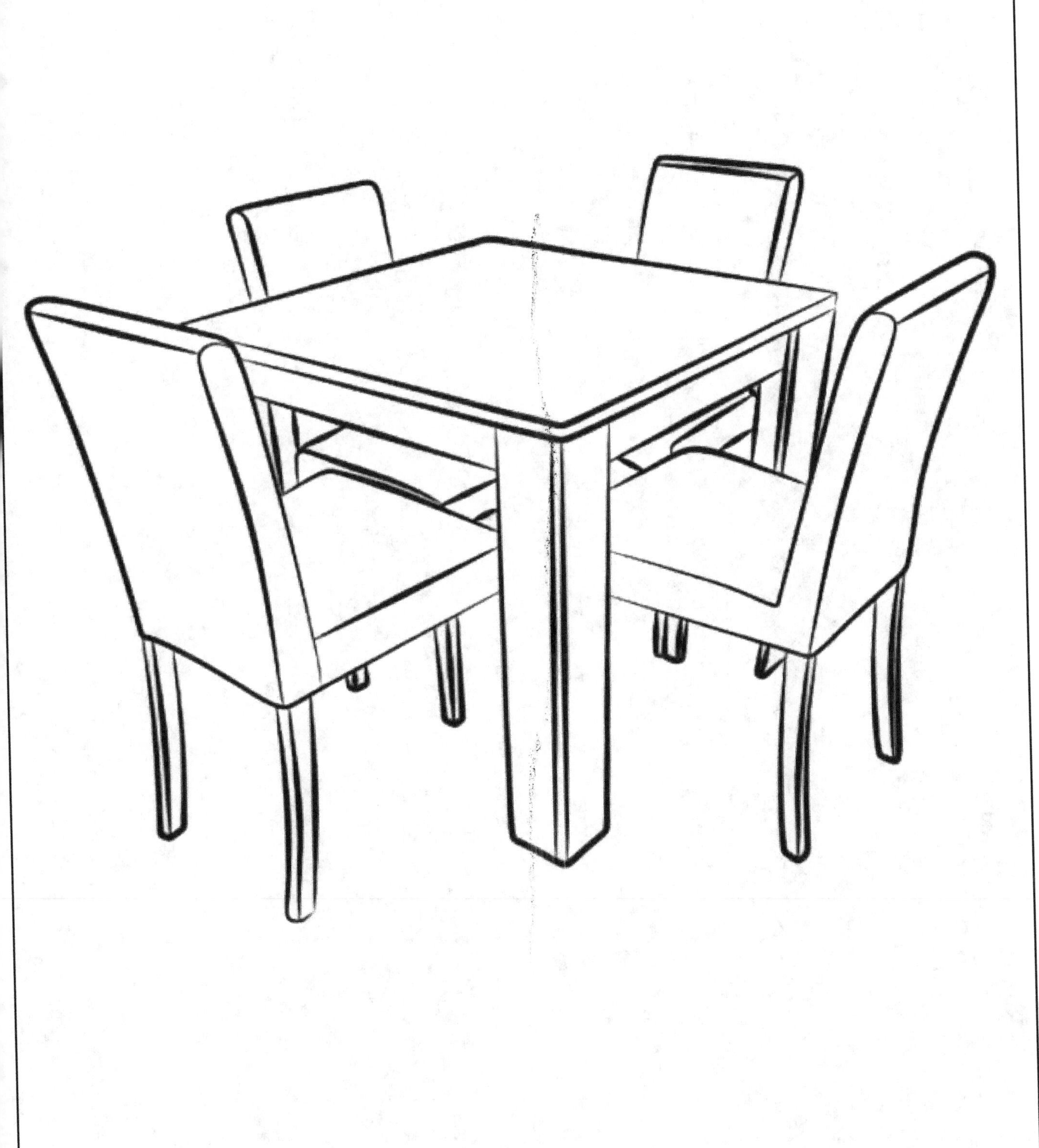

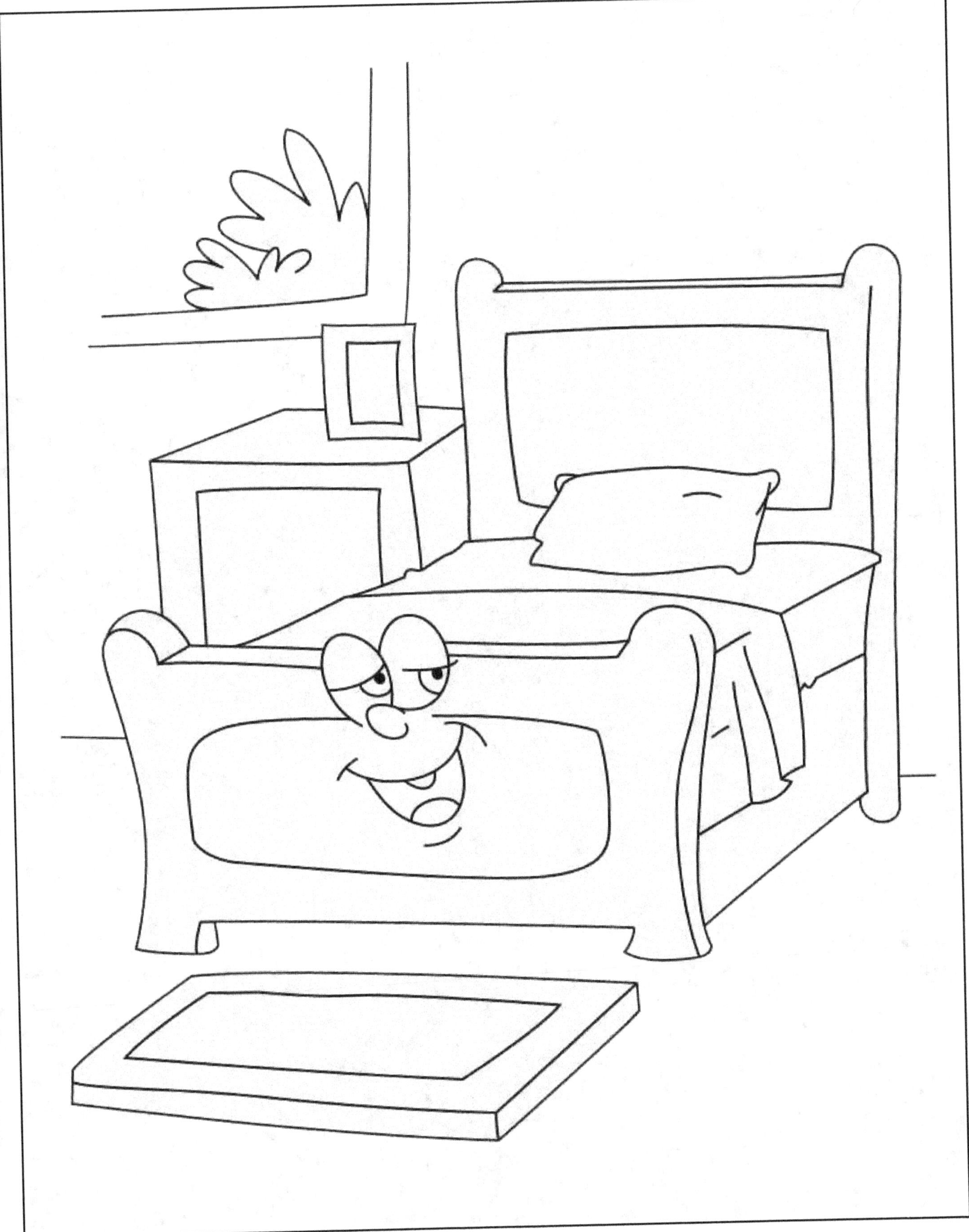

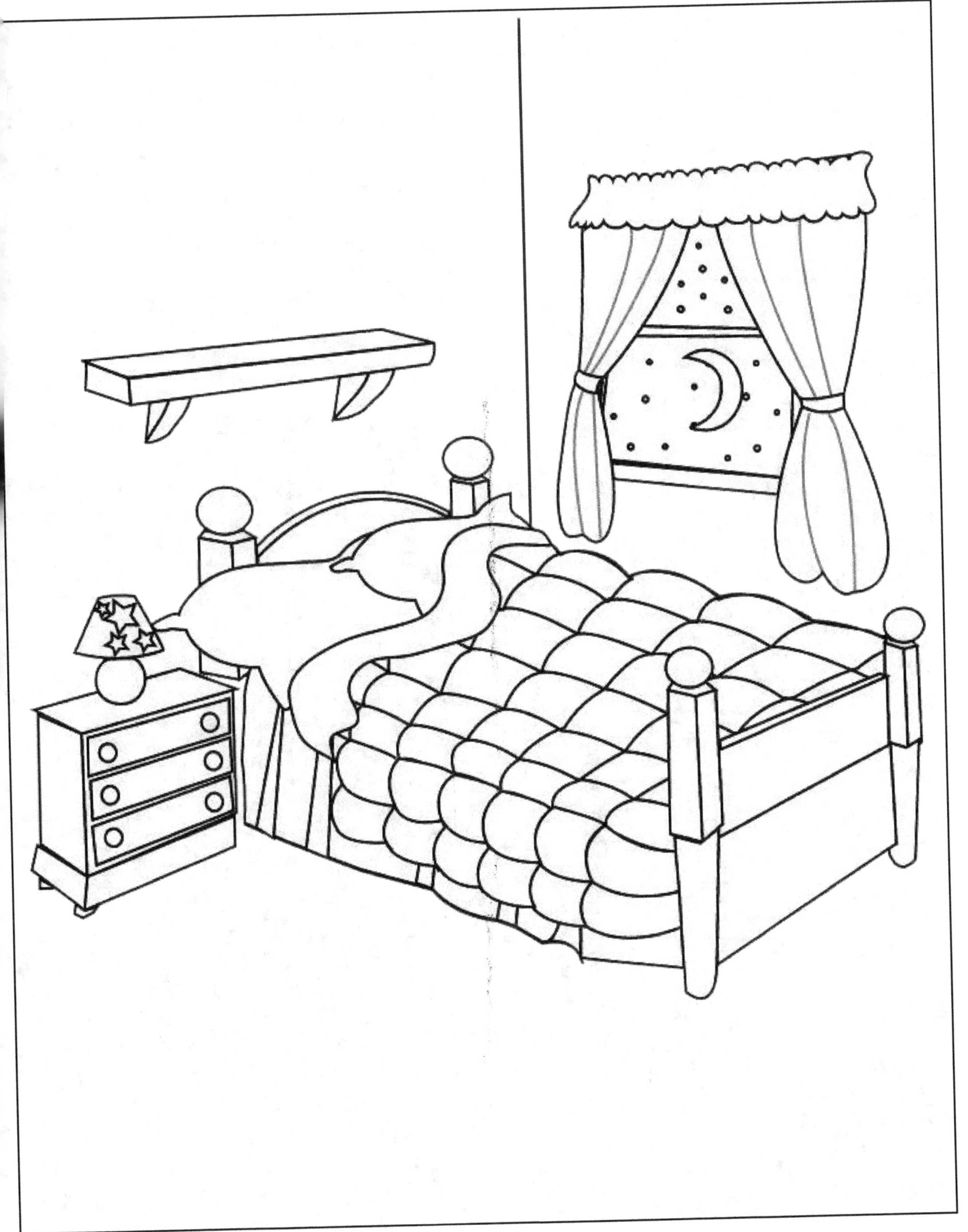

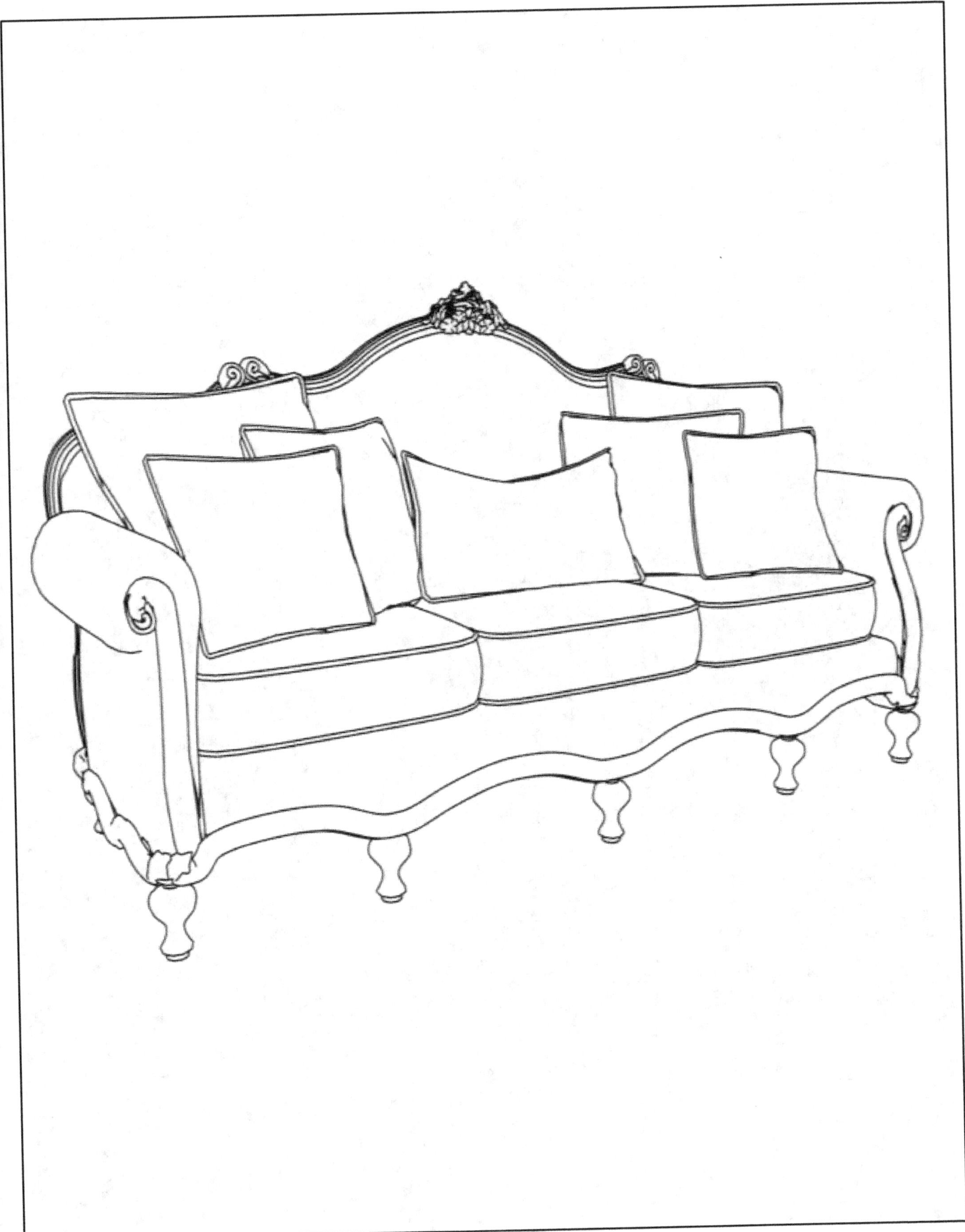

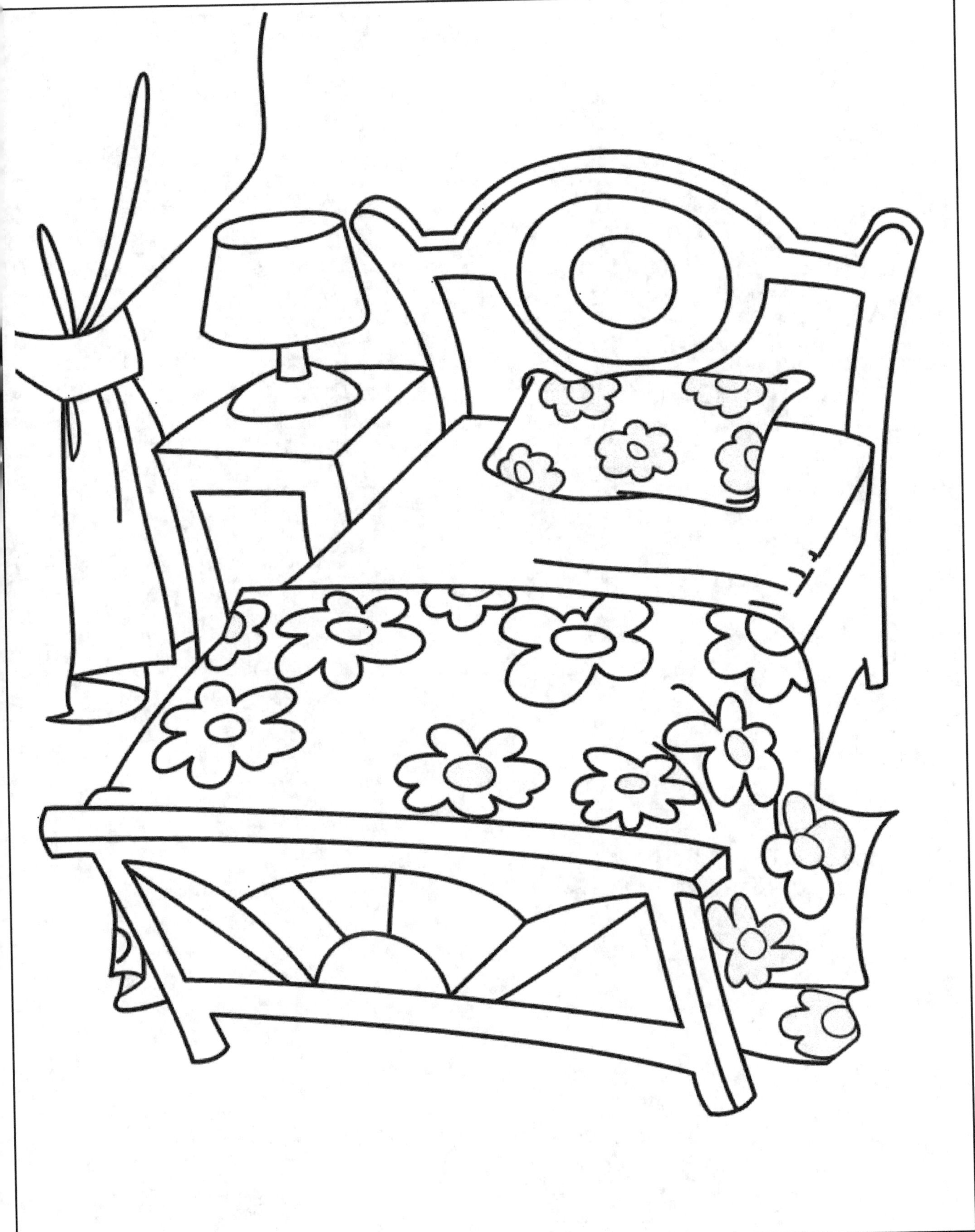

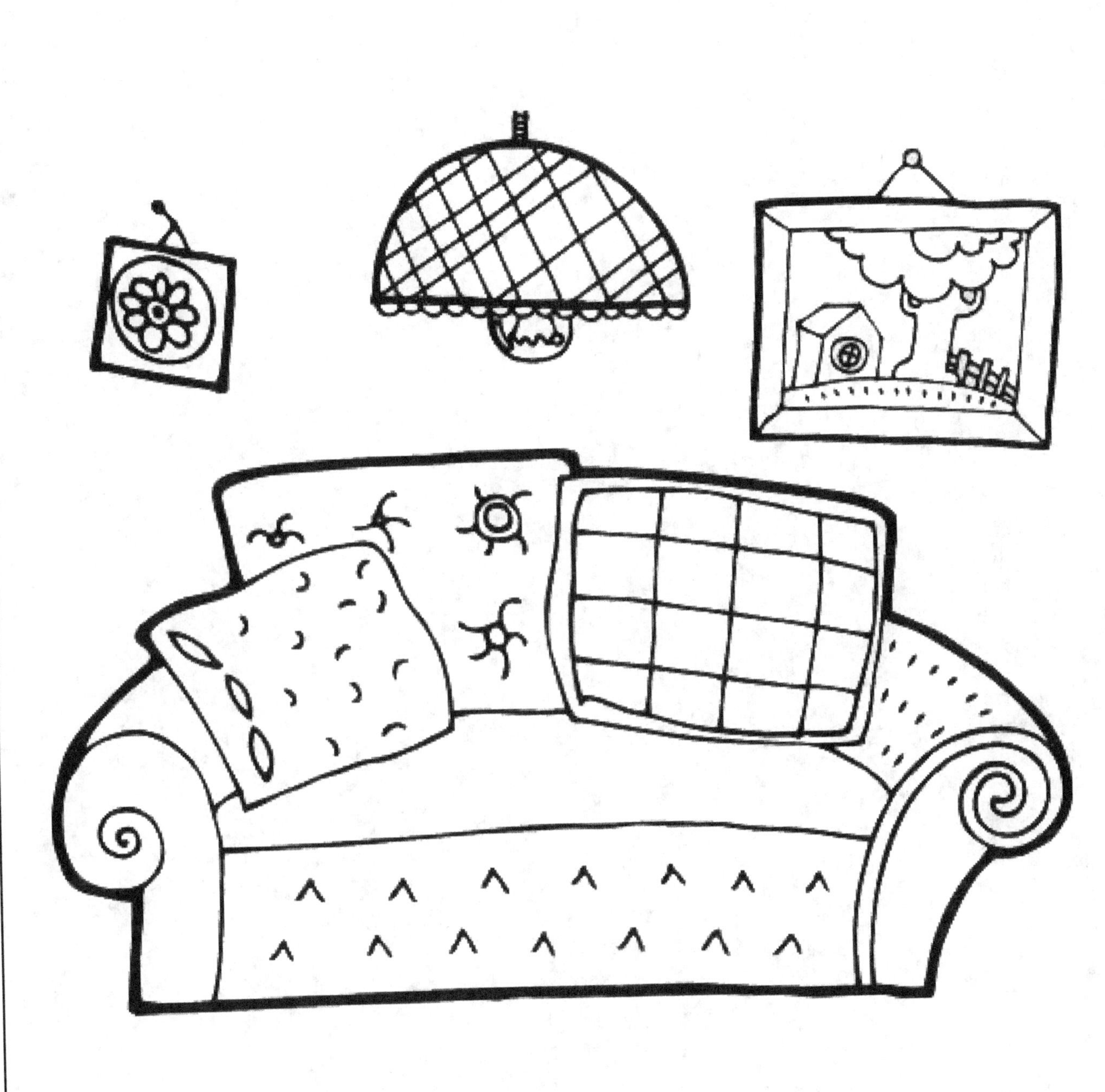

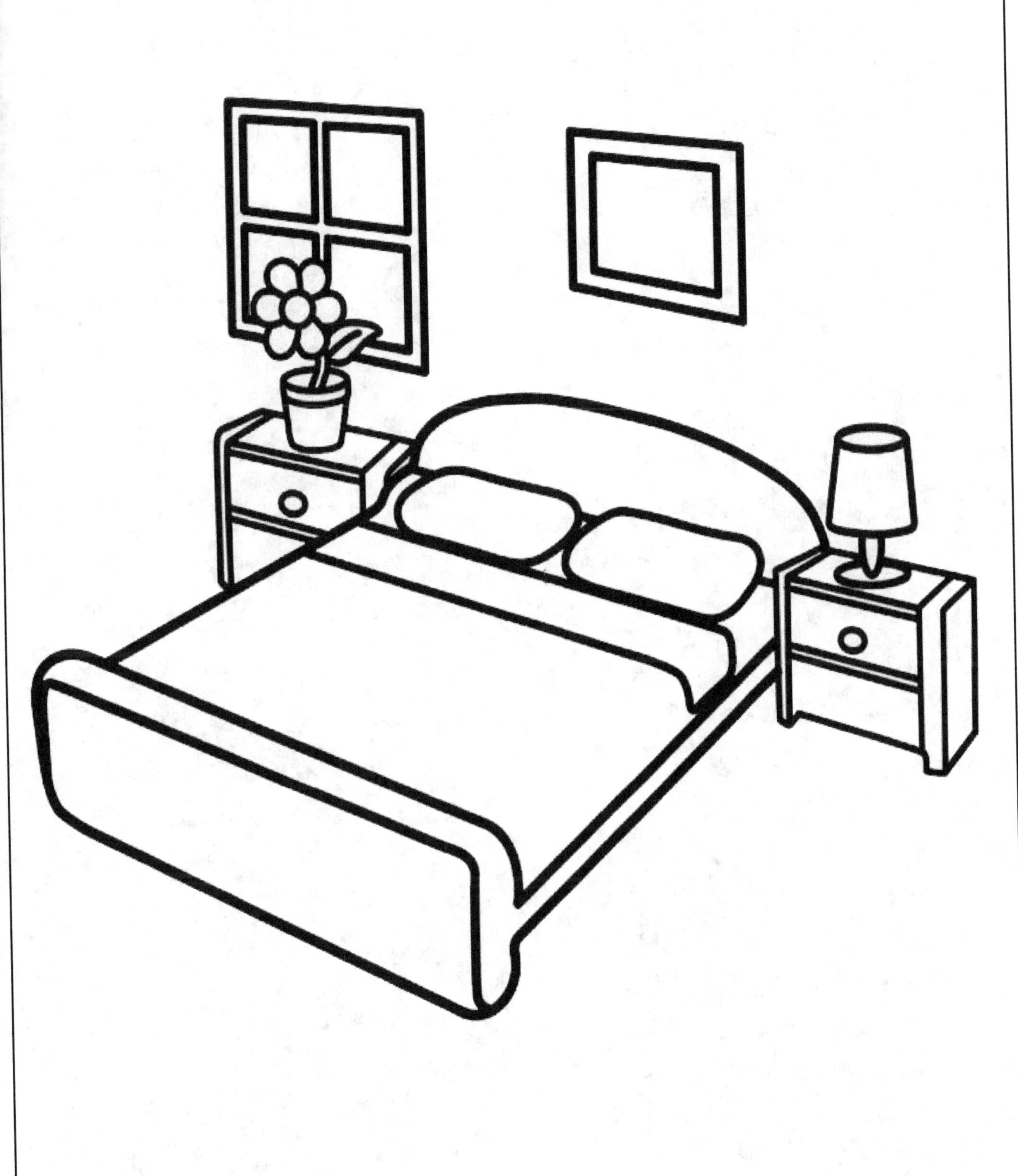

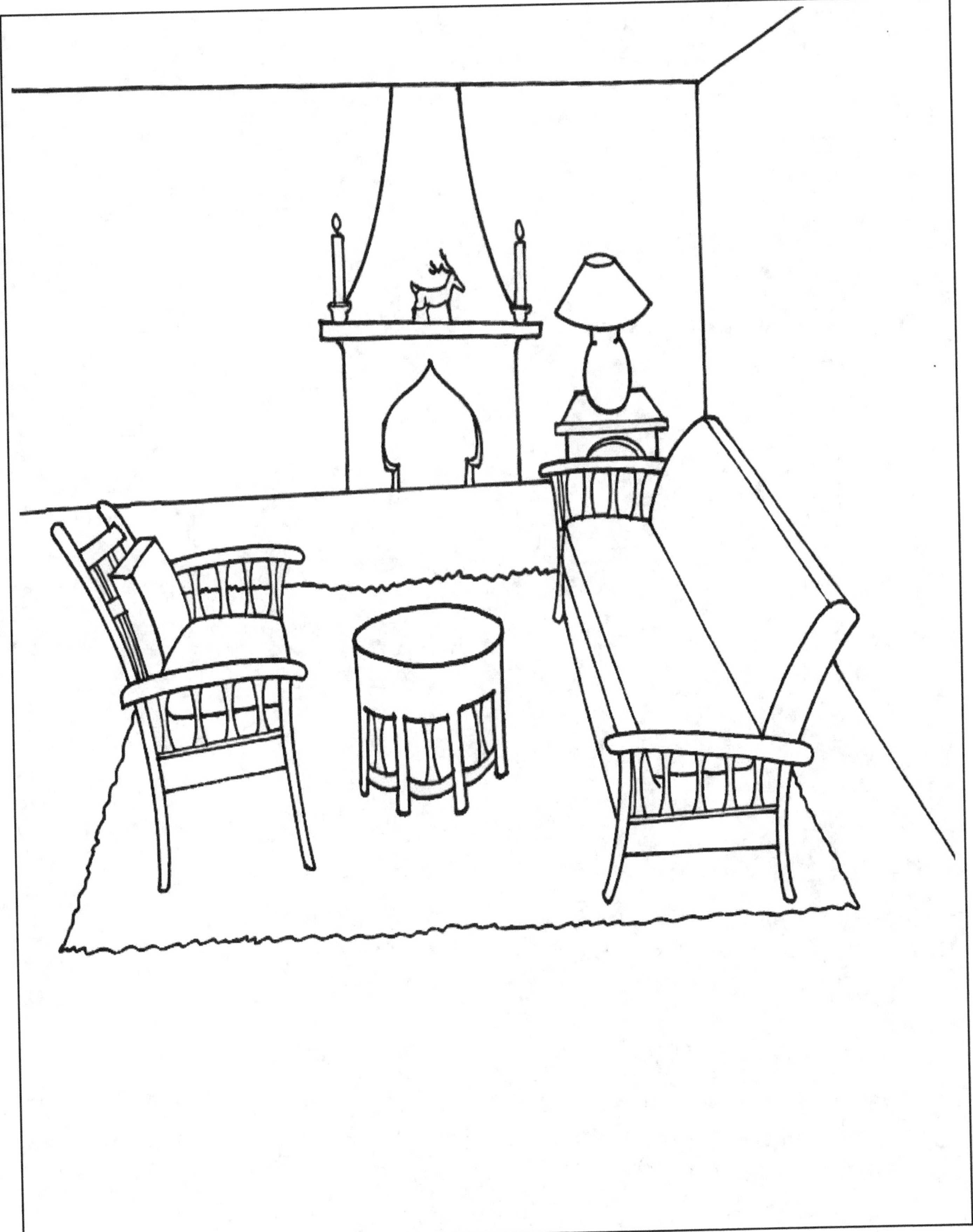